# WHAT LEADERS ABOUT *A SPIRIT-* CHURCH . . .

"*A Spirit-Empowered Church* is *not* just theory. Instead, it's practical reality. I had a front row seat (executive pastor) as Alton put these principles into action at First Assembly, North Little Rock. After thirty years of stagnation, the church grew into a strong, healthy, Spirit-empowered body of believers that tripled in size during Alton's fifteen years of leadership. You can only imagine how intimidating it was to follow him as pastor! But the journey that began in 1986 continues today. First Assembly still puts the same principles into action and has tripled again! I can't promise your church will triple, but if you put these biblical principles into action, they will breathe life into your church and your community. Regardless of size, context, or style, a Spirit-empowered church is a difference-making church! This is a Spirit-empowered book by a Spirit-empowered leader with practical ministry experience! Read it, pray over it, and apply it."

— Rod Loy, senior pastor, First Assembly of God, North Little Rock, Arkansas, author of *Three Questions*, *Immediate Obedience*, and *After the Honeymoon*

"Our twenty-first century world is filled with human conflict, religious stagnation, secular cynicism, and oppression by immorality. This sounds a lot like the first-century world that gave context to the early church and the book of Acts. Those first followers of Jesus impacted their world through the power of the Holy Spirit and intentional discipleship. In the book, *A Spirit-Empowered Church*, Alton Garrison provides a practical and inspirational way that first-century power and progress can be experienced in a twenty-first-century disciple-making church. Alton's biblical approach, inspirational insights, and personal stories make this a must-read for today's Spirit-empowered pastor."

— **Dr. Billy Wilson, president, Oral Roberts University and Empowered21; author of *Father Cry* and *Fasting Forward***

"Alton Garrison is the real deal— he's not just a theorist, but he's effectively led churches and movements to greater effectiveness. Now, he's taking the wisdom that's benefitted thousands of Pentecostal churches and putting it down in a practical and accessible book that will benefit countless more."

— **Ed Stetzer, executive director of LifeWay Research**

"Imagine how different your church and community would be if followers of Jesus made disciples . . . who made disciples . . . who made disciples! Drawing upon his own courageous and obviously anointed journey, my friend and colleague Alton brings us back to a Spirit-empowered discipleship process of 'loosing the laity,' which turned the first-century world upside down for Jesus. Allow God to use this insightful message to instill hope that His Spirit can do it again,  in your church, in our world, in our day. Read it and reap."

— **Dr. David Ferguson, executive director, Great Commandment Network; chairman, Empowered21 Global Task Force on Discipleship; author of several books including *The Great Commandment Principles* and *Relational Foundations***

"Alton Garrison is probably best known in the Christian family as a leading denominational executive of one of the nation's growing church movements, but in *A Spirit-Empowered Church*, he shares his challenges and achievements in the arena of the pastorate, and he establishes his credentials as a trainer of pastors. This is a book well worth reading—and mastering—by any leader interested in a church development plan that is biblical, practical, and proven. I will energetically recommend this book to any hungry-hearted pastor who wants to lead an Acts 2, effective congregation."

— Mark L. Williams, DD, presiding bishop/general overseer, Church of God

"If you are ready for your church to impact the culture with the gospel of Jesus Christ, *A Spirit-Empowered Church* is a must-read. Dr. Garrison clearly lays out from Scripture and from personal experience a path for healthy sustainable church growth. This is a book you will want to keep in arm's reach to gain continued insight as you lead, equip, and engage the next generation."

— Sam Rijfkogel, senior pastor, Grand Rapids First Church, Grand Rapids, Michigan

"Revitalizing plateaued or dying congregations is a major challenge for every Christian movement. Alton Garrison's inspiring account of how the Holy Spirit performed that in North Little Rock, Arkansas, provides a template of wisdom and hope for pastors called to such challenging assignments. There is hope in the power of the Holy Spirit! I will be advising pastors in our movement to carefully and prayerfully read this book."

— Dr. Doug Beacham, presiding bishop, International Pentecostal Holiness Church; author of *Plugged into God's Power*

"*A Spirit-Empowered Church* is an essential resource for leaders desiring to tap into the dynamics of the Acts 2 church. Drawing from extensive ministry experience, Alton Garrison has compiled a biblical blueprint of principles that enabled him to lead a plateaued church to dramatic growth. As a pastor to pastors, he has influenced healthy growth in many churches through this proven model."

— Kermit S. Bridges, DMin, president, Southwestern Assemblies of God University

"*A Spirit-Empowered Church* is an amazing tool for helping all churches discover their own cutting-edge culture needed to propel their development and influence. With vast personal experience and credibility, Dr. Garrison shares his own church leadership experiences while offering solid biblical principles to equip leaders for phenomenal growth. Of all the resources there are, *A Spirit-Empowered Church* contains the essential elements needed for your church to get real spiritual forward traction for the next level!"

— Robyn Wilkerson, copastor, Trinity Church, Miami, Florida; cofounder of Peacemakers Family Center; coauthor of *Inside Out*

"Alton Garrison lays out the simple truths to building an effective church in his newest book, *A Spirit-Empowered Church*. Not only does he take you through the spiritual principals of church building that can be found in Acts 2, but he teaches how to apply them to your ministry in a practical and effective way that has proven fruitful for him for over thirty years. Alton draws on the five biblical functions that are necessary for the church to become effective as outlined by Luke in the New Testament. With years of experience practicing these five principals, there is no one in ministry today more qualified to teach this breakthrough message than Alton."

— Matthew Barnett, cofounder of The Dream Center, Los Angeles, California; author of *The Cause Within You*, *Misfits Welcome*, *God's Dream for You*, and *The Church That Never Sleeps*

Alton Garrison

# A SPIRIT-EMPOWERED
# CHURCH

## AN ACTS 2 MINISTRY MODEL

Published by Influence Resources
1445 N. Boonville Ave.
Springfield, Missouri 65802
www.influenceresources.com

Cover design by Beyond Creative (www.beyondcreative.cc)
Interior formatting by Anne McLaughlin

Unless otherwise noted, all Scriptures are taken from the Holy Bible, New King James Version, © 1979, 1980, 1982 by Thomas Nelson, Inc., Publishers.

Scripture quotations marked NIV are taken from the 2011 edition of the Holy Bible, New International Version®. NIV®. Copyright © 1973, 1978, 1984, 2011 by Biblica, Inc.™ Used by permission of Zondervan. All rights reserved worldwide.www.zondervan.com. The "NIV" and "New International Version" are trademarks registered in the United States Patent and Trademark Office by Biblica, Inc.™

Scripture quotations marked NLT are taken from the Holy Bible, New Living Translation, © 1996, 2004. Used by permission of Tyndale House Publishers, Inc., Carol Stream, Illinois 60188. All rights reserved.

Scripture quotations marked CEB are taken from the *Common English Bible,* Copyright © 2011 by Common English Bible.

Scripture quotations marked TLB are taken from *The Living Bible,* Copyright © 1971 by Tyndale House Foundation.

Scripture quotations marked ESV are taken from *The Holy Bible, English Standard Version* Copyright © 2001 by Crossway Bibles, a publishing ministry of Good News Publishers.

Scripture quotations marked NASB are taken from *The Holy Bible, New American Standard Version* Copyright © 1960, 1962, 1963, 1968, 1971, 1972, 1973, 1975, 1977, 1995 by The Lockman Foundation.

02-7381
ISBN: 978-1-68154-001-6
21 20 19 • 5 6 7
Printed in the United States of America

# THE ACTS 2 MODEL

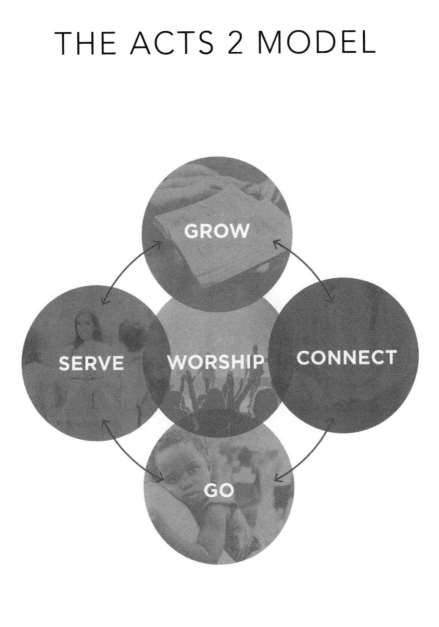

# CONTENTS

# FOREWORD

Forget Harry Potter and Hogwarts. We know very well that real spirits exist in the communities of the world today. The spirit of Pharaoh holds people captive in the Egypt of spiritual bondage and fear. The spirit of Goliath still mocks and intimidates the children of God. The spirit of Jezebel continues to make men and women hide in caves of sexual perversion and other unspeakable sins. The spirit of Absalom divides homes, churches, and relationships, while the spirit of Herod kills the young through abortion, violence, poverty, and sex trafficking, murdering good and godly young dreams and visions.

Yet there is a Spirit more powerful than these combined forces. In the midst of moral relativism, cultural decadence, spiritual apathy, and ecclesiastical lukewarmness, the most powerful spirit alive today is not the spirit of Pharaoh, Saul, Absalom, Goliath, Jezebel or Herod; the most powerful Spirit on the planet is none other than the Holy Spirit of almighty God, the Comforter indeed. As God spoke through the prophet, "'Not by might nor by power, but by My Spirit,' says the LORD of hosts" (Zech. 4:6).

Jesus didn't say, "Be touched, caressed, motivated or excited by my Spirit." Through Paul, He said, "Be filled with the Holy Spirit" (Eph. 5:18). Why? Because the Spirit of God empowers us to live in freedom (2 Cor. 3:17). He enables us to experience God's mighty power (Acts 1:8). God's Spirit equips us with the security of ever-present comfort (John 14:26), while enriching our lives with supernaturally sustained holiness (2 Thess. 2:13).

The opportunity to be filled with the third person of the Trinity requires immediate attention. All Christ-followers need to embrace one of the most powerful deliverables of a blood-washed, Spirit-empowered life. With righteous eloquence and prophetic articulation, Paul explained, "But if the Spirit of Him who raised Jesus from the dead dwells in you, He who raised Christ from the dead will also give life to your mortal bodies through His Spirit who dwells in you" (Rom. 8:11). In essence, the Spirit of God takes us from merely occupying space on this planet to a life overflowing with the fruit of the Spirit—from barely existing to truly living.

When Jesus asked His disciples who they believed He was, Peter didn't identify Christ merely as the Son of God. Instead, Peter declared, "You are the Christ, the Son of the living God" (Matt. 16:16). Why did Peter not just say "the Son of God"? Why did he add an extra modifier? The Holy Spirit directed his answer. We follow a living, communicating, empowering Savior, not a dead, buried, marble statue, museum-type God, but the "living" God.

Respectfully, the questions must be asked: If He is a living God, what kind of church should we be? What kind of families should we grow? What kind of language should we speak? What kind of thoughts should we have? What kind of lives should we live? Jesus gives us the answer: "I have come that they may have life, and that they may have it more abundantly" (John 10:10).

From the pages of Scripture to today's headlines, we understand that today's complacency is tomorrow's captivity. In other words, there is no such thing as comfortable Christianity. Dr. Alton

Garrison is my dear friend and the leading voice in Christendom on the crucial topic of discipleship. He profoundly and succinctly states, "A church exists to *connect, grow, serve, go,* and *worship.*"

A Spirit-empowered church—a living, holy, healed, healthy church—stands poised to build a righteous firewall and to empower believers filled with the Spirit to rise up with conviction and courage and declare: For every Pharaoh, there must be a Moses. For every Goliath, there must be a David. For every Nebuchadnezzar, there must be a Daniel. For every Jezebel, there must be an Elijah. For every Herod, there must be a Jesus. And for every Devil that rises up against us, there is a mightier God who rises up for us.

The church of Jesus Christ is not an ordinary institution. We aren't Google, Ford, Microsoft, or Starbucks. We are the church of Jesus Christ, empowered by His Spirit, and the gates of hell shall not, cannot, and will not prevail against us.

Be filled with the Holy Spirit!

— Rev. Samuel Rodriguez, President of the National Hispanic Christian Leadership Conference, Elk Grove, California

# INTRODUCTION

Jesus Christ is the hope of the world, and in a mark of His incredible grace, He has chosen us to be His partners in reaching, redeeming, and restoring a lost and broken world. The church isn't buildings, a business, or programs. The church is *people*—individuals who form a body. We are God's hands, feet, and voice to the people around us . . . and to the people around the world.

Each of us is part of that body, and together we have the mandate to carry out Jesus' final instructions while He was on the earth: go into every part of the world to share the good news and make disciples.

Alone, this is impossible. Together and empowered by the Holy Spirit, we are not only capable but also anointed to share the gospel with every people group on the face of the planet.

This book is about the church, but the church is made up of individuals just like you and me. It starts with one—just one person who decides to be a Spirit-inspired disciple of Christ, engaging in the Great Commission to reach people with the life-changing message of the gospel of grace and governed by the Great Commandment of loving one another.

You, friend, are the hope of the world because *you* are part of the church. Together, we will bring hope to a dying world as we *connect, grow, serve, go,* and *worship* by following the example the first-century church left for us in Acts 2.

# UNIT I
# OUR CHALLENGE

# 1 THE MISSING PROCESS

My dad was an alcoholic and a high school dropout. Before I was born, when he was thirty-seven, his addiction was ruining his life. When he and my mother learned she was pregnant—which the doctors said could never happen—it was a shock. They had been married seven years but had not been able to have children.

My dad was an oil field worker, and he had married a woman twelve years younger than he was. He had brought her into the lifestyle of an alcoholic, and over the years, he often lost his jobs because he couldn't control his drinking.

My dad had tried to quit many times and tried again when he learned they were pregnant—without success. Everyone had given up hope in my father and his many broken promises. He knew he was in no position to be a good father in his current condition, but he seemed powerless to change.

Shortly after learning they were pregnant, my parents were driving home from a July Fourth celebration. My dad had been drinking, and as they drove down the Texas country road, he suddenly began having chest pains.

His first thought was that he was going to die without ever having seen his child. His second thought was that he was having a heart attack, and while he was afraid to die, he was also afraid that he would die at the wheel and the driverless car would kill or injure my mother and the baby.

Without saying a word, he began to slow down to lessen the impact. He thought that if he died, he would slump across the wheel and the car would just stop. He didn't tell my mom a thing, but while clutching the steering wheel and sweating, he whispered a prayer: "God, I don't know how to pray, but my mother used to pray. If You heard her prayer, maybe You'll hear mine. Spare my life to see my child. Save me, and if I ever take another drop of liquor as long as I live, I want You to poison me and let me drop dead."

Dad had never kept a promise to stay sober, but in His mercy, God looked past all the prior failures and broken promises and saved him, healed him, and delivered him from alcohol addiction.

From that day forward, he never took another drink.

## MISSING THE PROCESS

My father was thoroughly and spectacularly converted to Christ and miraculously delivered from his alcohol addiction. But the transformation didn't end there. About six months after I was born, Dad was appointed the pastor of a small church—after being saved less than a year.

He had yet to preach a single sermon.

He and my mother pastored that small church in Sour Lake, Texas, for twenty-two years. During that time, God used Dad's salvation experience and a message He put in my father's heart to change lives.

My dad started his ministry with a supernatural experience, but he spent his ministry without seeing numerical success. I doubt if we ever had one hundred people in that little church even on Easter or during a great revival when the church was packed each night. You see, our church could only seat about ninety people!

My dad had a great appreciation for the Spirit-empowered message the church received at Pentecost. Dad was a pastor who understood the magnificent grace of God. He fasted and prayed; he was sincere and dedicated. He often taught about the power of the Spirit, and while he had an experience with Christ and had a message to share, he was missing something. It wasn't that he was doing it wrong; he just didn't have the whole picture.

What he lacked was a *process*.

I know what it feels like to try so hard but feel so confused. When I became pastor of First Assembly of God, North Little Rock, Arkansas, in 1986, I followed my dad's example. I had been an evangelist for eighteen years, I had the Pentecostal experience, and I had the message. When I shared my experience and began to preach a Spirit-empowered message, revival came.

But I was missing something.

I knew how to preach a sermon, how to bring people to the altar, and how to help my congregation be blessed, but for all that my father taught me, he didn't teach me how to take a church from where we were to where we needed to be.

Dad didn't have a process, and neither did I.

I didn't need a trendy, new, unique process for building a healthy church. I needed to look at what God had already done in establishing the very first church. I needed a complete Acts 2 church—not just the experience and message but also a process and a plan. In my ministry and in our church, I needed a process that would show us how a first-century church could effectively be reproduced in what was soon to be a twenty-first-century world. This realization and process changed many lives, including mine and many in the church I pastored and in the denomination I now serve.

As you pick up this book, you may be in the same place my father and I were. You are sincere, dedicated, committed, spiritual, and faithful, but you feel you lack something.

I believe many of us have missed a complete understanding of what the Holy Spirit did in the first-century church. The early church impacted the then-known world, walking out God's plan and doing the work of the ministry as a chosen generation and royal priesthood. Certainly it had some problems, but the first-century church turned the world upside down.

I'm convinced the church Luke describes in Acts 2 is the model, the plan, and the process that Jesus envisioned for the church on the earth.

The best part is that anyone can do it. It doesn't depend on the size of your congregation, your building, your town, or your bank account. It depends solely on our limitless God with whom all things are possible.

## THE ACTS 2 MODEL

In 1988, I began to put together my thoughts on a strategic process that eventually became the Acts 2 process. I'm not a very creative person, but I am conceptual—I can take an idea and flesh it out—and I developed the material that I discovered in Luke's account of the early church.

This process isn't something I've just read about; it's something I've *lived*. It's something I developed while leading a church that had plateaued for thirty years, and it all came together as I observed the five functions upon which Jesus founded the first-century church.

Jesus told the disciples to wait in Jerusalem "until the Holy Spirit comes and fills you with power from heaven" (Luke 24:49 NLT). Later He said, "You shall receive power when the Holy Spirit has come upon you; and you shall be witnesses to Me in Jerusalem, and in all Judea and Samaria, and to the end of the earth" (Acts 1:8). Then in Acts 2:4, they had a supernatural experience—Pentecost. In Acts 2:5–41, Peter went out to the inquisitive Jews and began to explain what was happening; he was preaching the message.

The content of the process God was birthing in my heart is found in Acts 2:42–47:

> And they continued steadfastly in the apostles' doctrine and fellowship, in the breaking of bread, and in prayers. Then fear came upon every soul, and many wonders and signs were done through the apostles. Now all who believed were together, and had all things in common, and sold their possessions and goods, and divided them among all, as anyone had need. So continuing daily with one accord in the temple, and breaking bread from house to house, they ate their food with gladness and simplicity of heart, praising God and having favor with all the people. And the Lord added to the church daily those who were being saved.

In this passage, the Holy Spirit began to explain the process of how to move from a temple model to a church model. Before Christ, the temple had been the center of life for the Jewish people. There, God's people read the Scriptures, prayed, encouraged each other, and worshipped God. The building was carefully constructed and ornately decorated. It was the place where heaven

> At Pentecost, an amazing and dramatic thing happened: Those who believed in Jesus became the place where heaven and earth met!

and earth met. The Holy of Holies was the inner sanctum where the Shekinah glory of God dwelled. But when Jesus died on the cross, the thick veil isolating the Holy of Holies was torn from top to bottom. The presence of God was unleashed and available to all who believe. Then, at Pentecost, an amazing and dramatic thing happened: Those who believed in Jesus became the place where heaven and earth met!

Decades later, Paul explained that our bodies are temples of the Holy Spirit (1 Cor. 6:19). Freed from a place, all believers and all gatherings of believers have become the place where heaven and earth meet—and all believers are now priests who love, serve, and worship God in all they say and do. Evangelism, discipleship, fellowship, ministry (service), and worship were to be the functions of an effective, Spirit-empowered church—they are the five functions upon which the Acts 2 process is based: *connect, grow, serve, go,* and *worship.*

## THE FIVE FUNCTIONS

A biblical, comprehensive, and strategic plan requires the empowerment of the Spirit to produce spiritual fruit in the lives of people. The plan is based on the five functions. The words describing the functions in Acts 2:42–47 are nouns, but because this is a process more than a destination, we converted them to verbs. These changes don't violate the mandate of the functions; in fact, they release the functions into action steps:

- **Connect**: fellowship and evangelism
- **Grow**: discipleship
- **Serve**: ministry gifts, outreach, building up the body, caring for the community
- **Go**: discipleship, evangelism, missions
- **Worship**: corporate praise, prayer, teaching, and singing

Let's take a quick look at each of these to frame our understanding of them.

## Connect

*Connect* focuses on the vertical and horizontal relationships in life. It begins with the process of salvation and continues through building spiritually strong relationships. Vertical relationship focuses on the process that connects people to God in all aspects of life. Horizontal relationship creates an atmosphere for relationship building person-to-person. Horizontal relationships consist of connections in every facet of life: family, church, local community, and global community.

## Grow

*Grow* is about discipleship. It's how your church promotes spiritual formation in the lives of individuals, ministry teams, and the congregation. It's about answering the following question: "How do we grow to be more like Jesus?" *Grow* centers on belief and behavior whereas *connect* is about the relationship.

## Serve

The Bible teaches that when we become children of God, He also makes us His priests to represent Him to everyone around us.

Many believers have never heard this magnificent truth, and their willingness and eagerness to serve is clouded by confusion and the desire for self-glory. Churches of every size need to move lay people from being spectators in the pews to becoming involved in the ministry of their churches. This is where the *serve* component comes in. As we help people learn about their gifts and abilities and what their passions are, we can help align them with ways of serving God and others that will be a good fit for them. *Serve* is about giving people outlets for the use of their gifts and abilities and giving them an opportunity to find their place in ministry.

## Go

*Go* is evangelism, reaching out to those who are next door and those on the other side of the globe. The evangelism component prepares and equips people to share their faith and accept the God-given mission for them and the local church. *Go* not only brings focus to the power of evangelism, but it also offers missional direction for individuals and the church body, including mission trips abroad and at home, long-term world missions, stewardship opportunities, relationship building with missionaries, and understanding the global perspective. It puts a great deal of emphasis on relational evangelism. This is where your church becomes more outwardly focused instead of staying inwardly focused, which is incredibly important.

## Worship

*Worship* is the intimacy and reality of the presence of Christ when leadership teams and the congregation see the character of Christ and the power of Christ connecting to individuals in their daily lives and corporately through the church family. Worship is far more than music, although that is a component. It includes prayer and powerful preaching.

These five functions provide the framework necessary to help us discover God's plan for how we handle fellowship, discipleship, ministry, evangelism, and worship.

## IT ISN'T ONE OR THE OTHER

These functions were the heart of God's original plan for the church. He had a plan—a process—but the plan was always and only to be carried out with His Holy Spirit's power.

Some leaders mistakenly assume it is an either/or proposition—either we are strategic and have a plan or we are Spirit-led and spontaneous. That's not correct; it's *both/and*. Some pastors don't like to plan, so they gravitate toward spontaneous spiritual expressions. Other church leaders become so focused on their plans they don't leave room for God's leading or His transforming power. For a church to be what God wants it to be, both are essential. The first-century church was empowered by the Spirit, but Jesus had a plan for those He was leaving behind. He *revealed* that plan through the power of His Spirit, and He *accomplishes* the plan through the Spirit's power.

Every church—small or large, urban or suburban or rural, American or international, and with whatever blend of ethnicity—needs both the power of the Spirit *and* a process of growth. Spiritual experiences are wonderful, but without a plan, you'll find yourself wondering how to take your church from where you are to where it needs to be.

The Acts 2 church had Jesus as its foundation and the Holy Spirit as its force. If we are to have healthy

> The Acts 2 church had Jesus as its foundation and the Holy Spirit as its force.

churches today, we need the same foundation, Jesus, and the same force, the Holy Spirit.

The power of the Holy Spirit is necessary for us to *be* more than we actually are. The anointing will help us *say* more than we actually know. The anointing will also help us *do* more than we can actually do. We need all of this if we are to effectively minister the gospel.

If we want healthy churches, we must embrace the source of power that enabled the first-century church to explode in the midst of fierce persecution. As it embraced these five functions under the empowerment of the Spirit, the church experienced exponential growth. As we have focused on these same functions, we have seen churches reinvigorated across the country. We have refined our own understanding of the process by working with hundreds of churches through what we call Acts 2 Journeys, which are multi-weekend experiences for pastors and their dream teams where we walk them through the Acts 2 process. We are seeing great results as pastors grow in confidence because they feel better equipped, their teams come together behind a unified vision, and their churches experience a profound impact. In short, what worked for the first-century church continues to work today because the Builder, Christ, used a sound blueprint when He founded the church in Acts.

The Acts 2 process in this book is for pastors and the members of their "dream teams"—the people in leadership at their church—to help them (and you) understand the process that my father and I and so many other pastors once lacked.

This book is about how to have a church modeled after the one Jesus founded—the same church that overcame incredible persecution to spread the gospel message to the then-known world.

The process God revealed to me out of Acts 2 is biblical, transferable, and replicable. It will work in rural areas, urban areas, and suburbia. It will work for large churches and small ones, healthy churches and unhealthy ones. Why? Because it isn't mine—it's the model Christ used originally. It worked for the church I pastored, and it has worked for many others.

It can happen in your church too.

# 2 CHANGE IS POSSIBLE

If you're reading this book, you want to create an environment for the people in your church to become healthy and to grow. Perhaps, you've been to conferences where experts told you how your church could grow, but the latest techniques had disappointing results. Or maybe your leaders have resisted your ideas and efforts in the past. Or maybe you're exhausted from trying so hard and seeing few results. Whatever the reason, you long for more. You want God to do something only He can do—in you and through you. You're ready for a more dynamic church. You're ready for more effective discipleship, a new outward focus, and the experience of the Holy Spirit's power. And you're ready to elevate and inspire helpers to become effective and committed coministers.

If so, you're where I was when God began to show me how His plan in Acts 2 made the first-century church so effective. There's only one problem: To embrace the plan God has for us requires something we typically don't like.

Change.

It took me two years to realize I needed to have the courage to change—I had to look for a process. I had to be willing to change the way I had been doing things. I had to trust God, but I also had to give a process time to develop and work.

One of two things will happen when we're confronted with the need to change. We either accept it, or we try to justify our decisions and resist it. Coming to terms with the fact that we need to change may be the hardest part of this process. The willingness to admit we need to do things differently is one of the biggest challenges we face in our Acts 2 Journeys.

It's the biggest obstacle standing in the way of renewal in your life and your church. Many leaders are convinced that the problem is the people, but the people aren't always the problem. We fear getting the people to change, but in reality, we're the ones who first need to experience change in our own lives.

We've seen what happens when leader after leader and church after church accepts their need to change and that the Lord is leading them into a process of renewal.

I was thirty-nine years old when God showed me I had to change. I didn't yet know what I needed to do, but God was about to show me the way. I accepted that I needed to make an adjustment, and God provided the resources to go forward. I believe that if I could find the courage to change, you can as well.

God offers each of us hope—hope that His dream for our future is greater than our memories of past ministries.

## DO YOU HAVE THE COURAGE TO CHANGE?

Know that right now, whatever your situation, you aren't alone. Your particular situation may be unique, but the problems we all face are actually quite common. We all struggle. We all have difficulties, setbacks, and storms, but through them all, it's imperative that we move forward. If we want to keep getting the same results we've had in the past, we can just keep doing what we've been doing. But if we want change to occur, we have to take wise, bold steps in a new direction.

> If we want new results, it's time to change what we do.

If we want new results, it's time to change what we do. That's what this book is about—the process of moving forward and the hope that things *can* change, as well as what Acts 2 has to tell us about those changes.

If you've tried to change before and failed, right now, you may be reading this skeptically. You may think that you've tried new plans, new programs, and new ways of doing things before—all of which may have failed or may have had less than earth-shattering success. I want to assure you that change is possible. Over the years, I've seen leaders from all kinds of churches who have found the courage to be objective about their current situations and to take bold steps to a better future. These men and women combined deep humility and the courage of a lion. They weren't willing to settle for anything less than God's best, and He gave them two crucial things: a deeper sense of His love and power and a clear, workable plan.

Trusting God's Spirit and following God's plan put us in touch with the mind and heart of God—we have revelations of His truth, the power to love and forgive, courage to speak truth, and humility to love difficult people. We no longer feel confused, and we no longer feel frustrated and helpless. Finally, we realize we aren't alone. We're in step with the plan and the power of God, and our vision attracts people who want their lives to count, also.

I know both sides of this experience. I've been there, and I've learned the lessons God wanted to teach me. Let me share with you what I discovered. It wasn't that I was doing something wrong; I simply didn't have all the pieces.

You may be in the same place I was—where many pastors have been—looking for the missing pieces and thinking change is impossible. Well, let me admit right away that what God is asking us to do—replicating the experience of the first-century church—*is* impossible. It's completely, totally impossible—if we rely on our own ingenuity, intellect, and human effort.

A look through the New Testament reveals contemporary examples of what God did with impossible situations. Every time God moved with wisdom and sovereignty, a new leader or a new process preceded it.

I'm not suggesting that your church needs a new pastor, but what I am advocating is that every one of us *can be* a new leader by embracing change. We can be transformed by the empowerment of the Spirit, and we can then change the atmosphere of our churches and congregations through the same plan that God used to transform the church of the first century.

Change is possible, friend. God did it before—He transformed Jewish believers into Christ-followers, and He can reinvigorate the churches of today with the power of the same Spirit that raised Christ from the dead.

## WHERE DOES CHANGE START?

I want to tell you about some of the obstacles to change I faced and how I got through them. It's easy to get the wrong idea about where change starts. It's easy to think it has to begin with the people and with the fear that we won't be able to get the people to change.

How many small churches in particular are led from the bottom up, administered from the pews? The pastor is to equip the saints to do the work of the ministry, but all too often, we have the incorrect understanding that pastors are paid to do ministry and everyone else is just there to help them. In reality, it's just the reverse, which we will talk about shortly in more detail in the next chapter.

> Only when this understanding of who is to do ministry is in place will we be able to empower our congregations.

In reality, members of the church board or some people in prominent families may resist change, but the paradigm shift begins with the leaders. Those in leadership must grasp what we call "the priesthood of all believers," and only when this understanding of who is to do ministry is in place will we be able to empower our congregations.

That's what happened with my own board at First Assembly in North Little Rock. After I had been there nearly two years, the vice chairman of the board at the church decided he didn't like that I was trying to move ministry from the pulpit to the pew by empowering the congregation as priests and co-laborers.

When I became pastor of First Assembly in 1986, we had a board of nine people. As many as nine months had passed between pastors, each of whom had lasted a shorter time with the church than the one before—a trend line that was alarming. My predecessor had only been there twelve months, the one before him thirty-six months, and the one before that sixty months. During this period, the board had become very hands-on, in effect, managing the church.

The vice chairman of the board was a man named Bill. He was a wealthy business owner who drove a very expensive car, and he had actually been instrumental in getting me to come to the church. While my predecessor had met with Bill frequently, I had not, and while we ultimately became friends, a crisis was developing. I knew something was wrong several months before he eventually confronted me, and I suspected that it was related to the strategic plan I was beginning to develop.

Having been an evangelist for eighteen years, I still traveled to speak occasionally, and the arrangement I had with the church regarding this travel and the materials my personal ministry continued to produce was a sore topic with him. He finally confronted me one night about this.

Actually, something other than my travel schedule or ministry resources was the real issue: Who would lead the church and where would it go? I was leading the church in a new direction, setting vision, and beginning to develop a strategic plan, but for years, the board had run the church. Bill was among those who didn't want to lose that power.

Would change happen? Would the direction God was leading me win out, or would the board continue to maintain the status quo?

"I think you misunderstood something," Bill said in this fateful board meeting. "We brought you here to preach, but *we* are going to run this church." He announced that they didn't appreciate my being gone or making money from the sale of my ministry's materials.

I asked him to unpack that a little for me, and Bill began to go into more detail about what he thought I was doing wrong and how I was wrong for what I was doing. When he was done, he said he wanted the rest of the board to share how they felt.

I told him, "No, you have told me how you feel. Now, I'm going to tell you how I feel. When I'm done, anyone else can speak."

I responded that their model of church governance was not preferable to my way, and then I told them why—it was unbiblical. I told them that I wasn't looking for a dictatorship but a collaborative effort. I shared my belief that God had designed a church to be led by a shepherd, not a committee.

Then I brought up the issue under the surface: As the pastor, I wanted to equip the saints for the ministry while Bill wanted me to be a hireling who performed the ministry for them.

"I'm willing to die for this church. Are you?" I asked Bill as I ended.

This discussion was heated because someone who had been in control now had that control threatened. Change threatened Bill and the rest of the board.

Before you think I'm some sort of aggressive, confrontational person, understand that I never raise my voice or bluster. However, I was fighting for the life of our church, and if I hadn't won that battle, that church would still be plateaued as it was when I arrived.

"Now, everyone can express themselves," I told Bill, "and if they feel like you do, tonight is my last night." In all my years of ministry, this was the only time I had thrown down the gauntlet and made this kind of dramatic statement.

That church wasn't going to become healthy and grow if change didn't start with the board. Let me tell you how that meeting ended. Everyone spoke, and they expressed themselves. Some began to cry, and it went from a confrontation into a prayer meeting.

A member who had been on the board over forty years and who was an advocate for me coming to the church had actually come out of retirement to be on the board and help me get started. He stood up after we had prayed and said, "I've been on the board over forty years, including twenty-two years when

Brother Gotcher was pastor. He was always the leader, he pastored the church, and we always helped him. This boy," he said, speaking of me, "is going to lead this church, and he's going to be the pastor. And we're going to help him."

Bill later shared with us at another board meeting that the night of that confrontation, he started to feel like he was going to die. He didn't know what was wrong, but he paced the floor and prayed intensely. He told us that God had said, "Take your hands off of Alton Garrison and stop trying to control him. If he has a problem and needs correction, I will correct him."

When I left the church fifteen years later, Bill apologized to me for what he had put me through. We became friends in the end, and what could have served to divide the church was instead a watershed moment for the church. Change had to happen, and I had to be willing to see it through.

God may not speak prophetically to the people who resist the change God wants to begin in you and your church, and you may not have an old saint in your corner to stand up in your defense. However, you must ask yourself if you are willing to put it on the line in order to usher in God's change for you and for your congregation.

The reality is that some board member or influential person in your church is going to resist change, and you must decide right now whether you are going to do it their way or God's way.

I'll ask you the same question I asked Bill: I was willing to die for the church I pastored—are you willing to die for yours? And perhaps even more pertinent is this question: Are you willing to *fight* for your church?

Let me ask it this way: Are you willing to lead, equip, model, love, sacrifice, convince, shepherd . . . and even fight if necessary . . . to see God change lives?

## FIVE KEYS TO CHANGE

God isn't intimidated by any problem in our churches, whether the challenges of rural churches, the struggles of urban society, negative trends in the culture, false religions, or anything else. So why should we let these things steal our hope?

So what exactly is a healthy church? Before we go any further, let me give you my thoughts on what that means.

A healthy church is a Spirit-empowered community of disciples who are following Jesus and fulfilling His mission. Healthy churches pursue and obey God passionately, engage and maintain loving relationships, develop and mobilize their people, act with clear direction and outward focus, and reproduce and multiply His mission in other peoples and places. We have determined that there are five things necessary for churches to experience revitalization:

1. *First is what we call a "burning platform," which is the crisis—it's the pressing need for immediate and radical change.*

Plateauing and declining churches, and the state of the church in the West in particular, are the burning problem of today. We have a crisis.

"Dying, Spirit-filled churches" should be an oxymoron, and yet all across America, we see churches in crisis.

God has a plan for each and every church, and we want to help church leaders find that plan and fulfill it. No church has a future unless its dreams are bigger than its memories, and we desire to help churches dream the dream that God has for each of them.

No church has a future unless its dreams are bigger than its memories.

The process of discovering that plan is what we have pioneered with our Acts 2 Journeys—programs that have helped literally hundreds of churches to discover and fulfill God's destiny for them.

While statistics support the burning platform, there is hope—your church doesn't have to become another statistic. Your church and its ministry have a hope and a future!

2. We must each be willing to admit we need help, create a community of leaders committed to helping one another succeed, and brave one of the most frightening words in the church: change. *This is the second critical element: equipping church leaders and pastors to thrive and grow—to change.* We fear getting the people to change, but in reality, change starts with the leadership.

> Sustained growth is a function of wise, godly, and visionary leadership.

Churches seldom outgrow their leaders. Some have accidentally grown beyond the capacity and vision of their pastor and leaders, but when they do, the growth is often short-lived. Sustained growth is a function of wise, godly, and visionary leadership. While not every church leader has the same potential, we can all get better—and we can all help one another do it.

To be better leaders, we must keep learning. There's no time limit on growth. We can keep learning until the day someone puts us in the ground. I've worked with leaders in their seventies who are still learning and growing, but sadly, I've also met pastors in their thirties who have stopped learning.

Jesus used some powerful analogies in His ministry—new cloth put on old garments and new wine poured into old wineskins. When we lose our capacity to grow, we run the risk of tearing and exploding when change comes. We must keep our elasticity—our willingness to change and grow and flex.

The purpose of the Acts 2 process is to enhance the capacity of every church leader to respond to the new wine of the Holy Spirit that God is giving His church. The process will show that change is possible and preferable, revitalizing leaders of all ages.

3. *The third critical item is the team behind every pastor—the volunteers and lay-leaders who make "church" happen every week.* No church can turn the corner without a great team of people working together and discipling new team members. They will do this when they understand the concept of the priesthood of the believer, which we'll cover in more detail in the next chapter.

Often, something is "lost in translation" when pastors attend conferences and try to transfer what they've learned to their ministry. They may come home excited and full of vision, but if a team of leaders doesn't share that vision and work together, but rather are at cross-purposes, it will be nearly impossible to implement the vision.

It's not enough to revitalize pastors; we must empower teams and help them understand that they aren't in the church only to be blessed but also to be a blessing to others. Leadership teams who engage in the Acts 2 process—working, praying, and dreaming through it together—will change churches. When you develop your understanding of God's plan and purpose as a team, the chances of success skyrocket. When church leaders work together with empowered teams, our experience shows that about 80 percent report significant progress.

The team-centered process doesn't end with the leadership team; the entire church must catch the paradigm shift that they haven't hired a pastor to do everything for them. They must grasp that all believers are a kingdom of priests and that congregation members are not helpers brought alongside a leader but are part of a team, serving God side by side.

The congregation members who see themselves as no more than helpers feel no sense of ownership, no vision for the future, and no drive to achieve great things for God. They won't take responsibility because they see themselves as helpers, not partners. When people see themselves as part of a team—all called to the same mission—they feel a sense of ownership.

The future of a church doesn't belong to one visionary leader. It belongs to a team of people who share a God-inspired vision for their church. Working as a team enables us to reach people for Jesus effectively.

4. *Fourth, it's critical that our churches become outward-focused.* No matter the size of our churches, we must fulfill our mandate: the Great Commission. For too long we have focused on making churchgoers comfortable. It's time to go into all the world with the gospel as colaborers for Christ, focused on the mission of winning souls.

This looks like marketplace evangelism—reaching people for Jesus through relationships. Healthy believers build relationships with people who need Jesus instead of expecting pastors to do it for them.

We are good at trying to witness with no commitment, no relationship. We can fill buses with people who will distribute tracts to people they've never met or put some people on a plane for a short-term missions trip, but when we ask people to share Jesus with those close to them, people they see every day, it's another story. We must move beyond the mild challenge of sharing our faith with a stranger we'll never see again to embrace the greater challenge of sharing Jesus with our neighbors, coworkers, and friends.

The most important number for your church isn't how many people attended last week but how many people in your neighborhood, town, or city need Jesus.

The most important number for your church isn't how many people attended last week but how many people in your neighborhood, town, or city need Jesus.

5. *The final critical component is a plan.* For too long, we've believed that the work of the Holy Spirit is only and always spontaneous. For too long, we've assumed that unless something happens on the spur of the moment, the Spirit isn't in it, but that isn't true. The Spirit of God imparts the plans of God, as well as the heart and power of God.

God has a plan for every church.

If He has a plan, why wouldn't He communicate it to us? We have the Holy Spirit as our teacher, and He revealed the plan to the church in Acts 2. Why wouldn't He share His plan with us for our churches?

He has, and He does.

We believe that a pastor and his core team of church leaders can sit and pray together and hear what God wants them to do *in the future*—the next service, the next month, the next year, and beyond. If we believe the Holy Spirit can speak to us in the moment, we must believe He can share with us the plan God has for our tomorrow. The plan doesn't come from a book. It comes from studying the truth of the Scriptures, praying together, and asking the Holy Spirit what He wants to do in and through us.

The Acts 2 Journey is my best idea of how to create a process where this plan can take root, flourish, and grow. It's the process my father lacked when he began his ministry and what I lacked when I began pastoring.

You won't find God's plan for your church printed for you in this book, but through the Acts 2 process, you'll develop a vision, you'll have renewed hope for positive change, you'll discover how to disciple co-laborers in Christ, and you'll find out how to receive a Spirit-led plan from God.

We've seen the fruit from churches that are being revitalized by making room for God and embracing the plan God laid out for the church in Acts 2. The leaders of these churches weren't content with the status quo; they didn't want to become irrelevant. Their days of mediocrity are over, and they are behaving as Spirit-led, Spirit-filled, Spirit-directed churches.

My hope is that you will become one of these churches, too.

# 3 THE PRIESTHOOD OF ALL BELIEVERS

In my first year at First Assembly of North Little Rock, I preached on a paradigm-shifting topic—the priesthood of all believers. This was the point of disagreement between the vice chairman of the church board and me—he believed they had hired me to do the preaching and ministry while they ran the church. Most of the rest of the people in the congregation had a role, too: to attend and give generously. I was the hired gun, and they were there to watch.

During my first year at the church, I preached fifteen weeks on a counter-cultural concept for our church: Ministry doesn't just happen from the pulpit but from the pews as well. Our board members, leaders, and attendees needed to progress beyond their current realities in Christ to become integral partners in ministry.

In Ephesians, Paul wrote that a pastor's responsibility is "the equipping of the saints for the work of ministry, for the edifying of the body of Christ" (Eph. 4:12). Though most leaders and churchgoers have never thought of it in these terms, they often expect that the pastor is the one doing the work of ministry. This assumption promotes the concept that everyone else in the church is just a "helper" who has no ownership or buy-in, as we discussed briefly in the previous chapter.

Many smaller churches experience this because the burden falls on the pastor and his wife to do *everything*. These "mom and pop" style churches put tremendous pressure on the pastor to do the work of ministry, and too many pastors think that church growth is the solution for this problem.

In reality, we need to change this paradigm—in ourselves and in our churches, no matter how large or small they are. While a bigger church may have a larger staff who feel they must do all the work of ministry by themselves, in point of fact, the staff should be equipping *God's people* to do the work, not doing the work by themselves.

The Bible teaches that we are a kingdom of priests. Peter wrote, "You are a chosen people. You are royal priests, a holy nation, God's very own possession. As a result, you can show others the goodness of God, for he called you out of the darkness into his wonderful light" (1 Peter 2:9 NLT). Preachers aren't modern priests; each believer has the indwelling presence of the Holy Spirit, and the entire congregation shares the mission of showing God's goodness to others.

The plumber in your church is a priest; plumbing is what he does to support his priesthood. The accountant is a priest; accounting is what she does to support her priesthood. Each believer is part of a royal nation and is called to "full-time ministry," even if they aren't *paid* full-time ministers. All of us should be living out our ministries on a daily basis.

When ordinary churchgoers catch the revelation that they don't come to church to receive ministry but to minister, this incredible paradigm shift causes churches to explode with life and health! We are all priests, and priests don't come to the temple to be blessed—they come to minister. Because of God's goodness, we get blessed as an ancillary benefit of coming to church, but the primary purpose of every priest in your congregation is to minister to those who are far from God.

> We are all priests, and priests don't come to the temple to be blessed—they come to minister.

Jewish priests had to pack up and move the Tabernacle, slay and butcher the sacrifices, and clean up the blood afterward. It was dirty, gruesome, difficult work. Modern priests have responsibilities as well—inviting friends and co-workers to church, greeting visitors warmly, serving the next generation in children's programs, and doing whatever else it takes to do the Lord's work.

Believers come to church to be blessed and ministered to, but that isn't the end of the story. Like Abraham, they are "blessed to be a blessing" in the lives of everyone they meet. Jesus explained the principle of overflow at a feast in Jerusalem. Each day of the weeklong event was a rising crescendo of sacrifices and washings. John explains this:

> On the last day, that great day of the feast, Jesus stood and cried out, saying, "If anyone thirsts, let him come to Me and drink. He who believes in Me, as the Scripture has said, out of his heart will flow rivers of living water." But this He spoke concerning the Spirit, whom those believing in Him would receive; for the Holy Spirit was not yet given, because Jesus was not yet glorified. (John 7:37–39)

When you and the people in your church catch this principle, it's an incredible ray of hope and a source of strength because you'll no longer feel alone as a minister. As you teach this and the people grasp it, you won't be surrounded by "helpers"; you'll be surrounded by an increasing number of "priests" who are overflowing with the love, forgiveness, and power of the Spirit! People who buy into this will feel a greater sense of ownership than ever before, and it will transform the way you do ministry.

The people don't exist to help the pastor; the pastor exists to help the people fulfill their callings. That calling for each and every Christian includes the Great Commission, which is the mission and purpose of the church and every part of the body of Christ: "Go and make disciples of all nations, baptizing them in the name of the Father and of the Son and of the Holy Spirit, and teaching them to obey everything I have commanded you" (Matt. 28:19–20 NIV). This mandate isn't just for pastors; it's for every believer.

This concept of the priesthood of all believers is the catalyst for every other component of the Acts 2 model. None of it will work without this shift of perspective; otherwise the pastor will have helpers instead of co-owners of the church's mission and vision. What Acts 2 asks, you can't do by yourself as a church leader—you must have the people with you. It's absolutely essential to grasp this concept yourself and to teach it as long as it takes for the people to get it.

Something amazing will happen when the people really buy in. If you catch nothing else that I've learned, hold on to this and watch it transform your church and your ministry.

## MANY HANDS

When I began pastoring First Assembly of North Little Rock, it was a church of about 500 people, and a few of them did all the work. Beneath the surface of my travel and ministry resources, the confrontation with Bill and the board was precipitated by my fifteen weeks of preaching that the people in the pews were a kingdom of priests and needed to be ministering.

By the time I left, the church had tripled and perhaps a thousand of them were involved in service of some sort. I would never have gotten so many people to buy in and get involved if the concept had persisted that I was hired to preach and do all the ministering, letting the board run the church.

This foundational biblical principle has changed more churches than just the one I served, and it's a central component in setting up the Acts 2 process. You won't get a sense of ownership from co-laborers who share your vision unless people understand that it's more than simply volunteering: It's a biblical mandate.

When you have a church full of people who are all about themselves and their preferences, their

> When you make the leap and people understand they're supposed to be contributors and not consumers, everything changes.

only consideration is their personal comfort and care. When you make the leap and people understand they're supposed to be contributors and not consumers, everything changes.

People who are consumers come to church, and they may participate in many activities, but they're cisterns that continually have to be filled. They aren't springs of water that are a constant source of nourishment for others. What turns a consumer into a contributor and turns a cistern into a fresh spring? The gospel of grace. When people are thrilled that the God of the universe loves them so much that He sent His Son to die in their place, they realize He is their greatest treasure . . . and they are His greatest treasure. A deep, compelling grasp of God's magnificent grace isn't just an entry point to the Christian life. It's the source of our deepest contentment and our highest motivation for everything we do each day. The grace of God humbles us because we realize our sins required the God of glory to pay the ultimate price for us, and it raises us to the stars because He loves us so much that He was glad to do it. This realization changes everything!

As people love and serve out of overflowing hearts, they will have the joy of seeing God use them to mend broken hearts and lead lost people home to God. Suddenly, "sacrifice" becomes a privilege, and people give more time and money because their hearts have been transformed. When people become contributors, the jobs of leaders change. We have the responsibility to place them in roles where they can be effective and then equip them so they can thrive. We help them find "the sweet spot" of their desires to serve in a particular role, their God-given ability, and an open door of opportunity.

However, not everybody who sits in church will grasp the wonder of God's grace and be transformed to become contributors. Some will remain consumers, no matter how beautifully and powerfully you explain the grace of God to them. In fact, some of them will resist your message of God's love, forgiveness, and power. Be aware: People who are only about themselves may head to the next feeding trough when you no longer cater to their whims. They aren't your responsibility. Your job is to equip the saints for the work of the ministry.

However, those who buy in will find that God provides an amazing side benefit when we serve—a serendipitous blessing.

While this isn't supposed to be our sole motivation, those who have this paradigm shift will find that it's incredibly rewarding.

In the chapter on the Acts 2 function we call *serve*, we will develop other aspects of this further, such as helping people find their spiritual gifts and discovering where they are best suited. First, we needed a biblical foundation, because this shift in thinking must come before we discuss the rest of the Acts 2 process.

One final element of the priesthood of all believers I would like to cover, however, is that while you won't pay these priestly volunteers, you must create a culture of accountability. At a job, someone can be fired for poor performance. I've found it helpful to have ministry agreements with those who serve that describe what is expected of them so that if any correction needs to take place, you have clearly defined parameters and can have constructive conversations. When you give people your expectations up front, they understand what they need to do and can decide if they are committed to meeting them or not. Also, I always provide a sunset—a time frame for their service and a reevaluation. At this time, we go over the ministry agreement and see if that avenue of service is a good fit.

Many smaller churches we work with haven't thought of this, worrying perhaps that it might deter volunteers when they are desperate for people to serve. I understand this, but I believe the clarity of communication that will come later is worth it.

A pastor of a small church came up to me after I had advocated asking volunteers to sign ministry agreements. He said, "You got me in trouble!" I asked him what he meant, and he told me, "Well, when I began teaching that volunteers needed to be faithful in attendance and faithful in tithing, a lady in the choir came unglued! She said I couldn't force her to do that—she had been there for twenty-five years!"

I asked, "Did you tell her it was a biblical principle?"

He said, "No, I didn't get to that."

"Did you tell her that you're trying to create a new culture and explain the priesthood of all believers?"

He shook his head. "No, I didn't tell her that."

I asked, "Well, what did you tell her?"

"I told her that you made me do it," he replied.

This is an amusing story that gets a laugh when I share it, but the reality is you can't just tell people that I told you to do it. You must believe strongly enough that you are training a kingdom of priests—and that as such, there are some reasonable expectations—if you want to create a new culture of service and ownership in your church. This can be done in a nice way; there's no need to be demanding or dogmatic. You may need to grandfather in some of your older saints, but you can teach the new people what you expect from your "priests." They will thank you for the clarity, and you will be glad for it, too, if you ever need to correct or guide them.

Holding people accountable in a church setting is different from a business environment. The volunteers at a church need direction and encouragement with gentle correction when necessary. Paul wrote to the Christians in Thessalonica, "Now we exhort you, brethren, warn those who are unruly, comfort the fainthearted, uphold the weak, be patient with all" (1 Thess. 5:14).

Teaching the biblical concept of the "priesthood of all believers" can easily be augmented with a simple visual illustration. The leadership triangle shows how our rights (options) decrease as our ministry (volunteer) responsibilities increase. To become more engaged in ministry opportunities results in limiting one's options out of love for God's work.

## OPTIONS DECREASE AS RESPONSIBILITIES INCREASE

**RIGHTS**

Remember, the key is that as a leader, you aren't there to do all of the ministry. Your primary role is to equip the saints for the work of ministry so that they edify the body of Christ. When you help your people with this paradigm shift, watch out—your church's ability to minister will explode, just as it did for the church of the first century.

# 4 HOPE

Church leaders who have a blend of a workable plan and the Spirit as power have a strong hope that their labor is not in vain—God will do something wonderful through them. However, I often meet with pastors who have lost hope. The causes are many and varied. They experience financial difficulties, family trouble, leaders' resistance, health problems, and discouragement from countless other causes. Our armed services have observed the devastating effects of combat fatigue on soldiers, and many church leaders suffer from a similar condition, sometimes labeled "compassion fatigue." It's the result of giving, serving, and helping without replenishing the necessary love, joy, and strength all of us need to keep going. If the trend isn't identified and reversed, it can lead to burnout.

All of us have ups and downs, depending on many factors in our personal lives and ministries, but if we dig deep enough into the power, presence, and purposes of God, our hope will be renewed.

Johanna and I were invited to speak for an exciting young pastor, Glenn Epps of Puxico, Missouri. When he had first arrived, the church had perhaps sixty people. He had been there for seven years, and it was now running about one hundred twenty. When he arrived, the average age was sixty-five, and it was now about forty. I was impressed because this was the most energized church in the county. There was just a buzz about the place. Young couples were everywhere, and everything just seemed fantastic.

At a luncheon afterwards, I asked him how he did it. He looked around at his people and then back at me before saying, "There are a lot of strategies out there, and I'm sure we've implemented a few of them. First of all, what I found to be the most important was that people had to understand I was here to stay. They needed to know I was called to this place, not just stopping off on my way to somewhere else. In rural America, if they don't think you're authentic and really love them, they won't work with you.

"Second, my biggest challenge was lifting the morale. They'd come to the conclusion that God couldn't help them and neither could anyone else. They thought they were just going to be stuck where they were. We didn't see people coming in. No one was excited, and no one was witnessing. Morale was our biggest issue."

I asked him what their biggest issue is today.

"Morale," he replied.

I told him, "I thought you said that was your biggest issue seven years ago?"

"I did," he said, but it's for a different reason now. Two years ago, the wife of one of the board members contracted a horrible, flesh-eating bacteria that doctors didn't immediately diagnose, let alone treat. She died, and because she was such a big part of the community, it seemed to suck the life out of people. They just lost hope."

I thought about how often I've preached on the subject of hope. When he had mentioned morale, I had been going back to some of those thoughts in my head. I was amazed that even in this vibrant, healthy church, morale was his chief issue.

We know faith is a process—faith comes by hearing and hearing the Word of God. The more Scripture you get inside you and the more you believe it, the more faith you will have. Faith is almost educational in nature.

But hope is emotional. You can't educate people into hope. Yet even in our darkest moments of disappointments and heartache, the Spirit of God can renew our hope. Paul explains, "And not only that, but we also glory in tribulations, knowing that tribulation produces perseverance; and perseverance, character; and character, hope. Now hope does not disappoint, because the love of God has been poured out in our hearts by the Holy Spirit who was given to us" (Rom. 5:3–5).

Faith is related to miracles, and hope is related to morale. It's that confident, happy expectation that something good is going to happen.

When I see churches that are plateaued or declining or when I meet a leader who feels unappreciated and can't get anything going, I know their hope tank is on empty.

What they need is a dose of hope.

Roughly a million people are worshipping every Sunday in Assemblies of God churches that are plateaued and declining, and they are good people—faithful people. But they have lost their hope.

Can we give it back to them?

I believe we can infuse demoralized people and churches with hope because it's a scriptural principle. So how do we do it?

Romans 15:13 says, "Now may the God of hope fill you with all joy and peace in believing, that you may abound in hope by the power of the Holy Spirit."

Who is the source of our hope? *God.* His autobiography, the Bible, tells us all we need to know of His character. His past

If the source of hope is God and the substance of hope is faith, the supplier of hope is the Holy Spirit.

performance is an accurate predictor of His future behavior.

If the source of hope is God and the substance of hope is faith, the supplier of hope is the Holy Spirit.

## A PERSONAL STORY OF LOST HOPE

My father's life and ministry were punctuated with dramatic miracles, so when he contracted Alzheimer's, we expected that we would pray and he would be healed. However, that's not how it happened. Over time, his condition got progressively worse. His slide from reformed alcoholic and vibrant pastor to unresponsive Alzheimer's victim was a journey of about eight years, and we understood as a family why some have called this period "the long good-bye."

Near the end of that eight-year journey, I was called to the hospital and happened to meet Dad's doctor as he was walking out of my father's room. He reiterated to me that my father's condition meant he would never speak to us again—his brain function was gone. In fact, he hadn't spoken intelligible words in several years and for over three months had not even made a single sound.

This was nothing that I didn't already know, but what he said next was what grabbed my attention. "It isn't your father I'm concerned about. We'll keep him comfortable until he passes. I'm more concerned about your mom. She's been his caregiver through this whole journey and she is physically, mentally, emotionally, and spiritually depleted. She needs help."

With those words, he walked out. I went into the hospital room and stood at the foot of Dad's bed. He was unchanged from the last time I had seen him. It was hard to see him in that condition, though—he had been such a healthy person. At six feet tall, he was now an eighty-seven-pound, emaciated figure curled into a fetal position.

I've seen miracles. I've witnessed firsthand the results of great faith, but when my own father needed a miracle, none seemed forthcoming. I had no hope left for my father's recovery.

I was worn out from being on an emotional roller coaster, and I didn't know how to respond to these condemning thoughts—except for quoting Scripture. I stood there wrestling with these thoughts and quoting every relevant verse I could remember. I would feel better for a few moments, and then the circumstances that confronted me would make me feel worse again.

Finally, I fought through and received victory in that fight. I said, "Devil, you cannot win! When my father dies, the tabernacle will perish, but his soul will live forever! He will be in the presence of the King of Kings and Lord of Lords!"

I walked out in victory to see my mom and sister. They had heard me inside, and my mom asked, "Son, what have you been doing?"

"I've been praying with Pop," I told her.

Her reply surprised me. "Why?" she asked. She had a look on her face I had never seen before. "It won't do any good—we've prayed for him for years and look at him. He is so bad, not even really there. His body has outlived his brain, and we can't communicate with him. There's no dignity in that room. I've been praying for God to release him, let him go to heaven. There's no reason for him to linger here, but he lingers on."

Then she said something I never thought I would hear: "When you need God the most, He turns His back on you. It's a joke; that's what it is." Pointing her finger at my face, she said, "Don't ever pray in my presence again!"

You can't imagine the impact her words had on me. Had my mother lost her salvation? Had she walked away from her faith? This was my mom—a faithful pastor's spouse for decades and a prayer warrior. She had walked with my dad through all the years and all the sacrifices during their years of ministry. Hearing her say those words was frightening.

I didn't know how to answer her; I simply walked away. Back in my car, I began to pray, simply venting to God. Finally I blurted out, "God, You have got Yourself a big, big problem. What are You going to do?"

I was afraid my mother had lost her faith. But she hadn't lost her faith—she had lost her hope.

## A CHURCH IN DECLINE?

How many believers are like my mother? For many church leaders, it's not a loved one's sickness that has sapped their hope; it's the state of their churches. Some are thriving, but the workload is crushing the pastor. Others are stagnant, and it takes all the pastor's time and attention to keep them from declining. And a few churches are in the process of decline. In my denomination alone, about two-thirds of the churches have plateaued or are declining.[1] Many of these churches have been beaten down and have lost their passion. They may have had fifteen pastors in the last twenty years. They've lost hope.

A look at the church worldwide may make many leaders stop and ask some hard questions that seem to have grim answers. It's easy to hear the Accuser's voice saying the church is no longer relevant to our postmodern culture, that new generations will no longer fill sanctuaries as their parents did, and that secularization will see people walk away from their faith. Some may say there is little hope.

For many church leaders, the conventional wisdom is that growth is the default indicator of a church's health. After all, a healthy church is growing—and eventually a growing church will increase in numbers and spiritual vitality. That's the nature of growth: Healthy plants and animals inevitably grow, but unhealthy plants and animals decline and eventually die.

God invites you and your congregation, regardless of size, to share a mission that matches both the mission field where He has placed you and the strengths with which He has blessed you, regardless of church size. Unlike many church leaders, He isn't obsessed with size as a measure of the effectiveness of a church. He desires small churches to be healthy just as much as He desires big churches to be healthy, and He desires that all churches be full of hope.

## LOOKING FOR HOPE

The church is the body of Christ, and Christ is the hope of the world. If we lose our hope for the future, what possible chance does the world have?

Remember the story of my mother's lost hope, for we'll come back to it later at the end of the book. The question I had within my spirit was whether or not she could find hope again. And this is the same question we must ask of the church. Within this book, we'll try to provide some answers to that question.

While this book is an exploration of hope for the church, it isn't a grim tide of numbers and statistics we must fight against. The fight is for *hope* itself.

We have *not* passed out of relevance, attendance in our congregations around the world is *not* doomed to decline, and future generations *will* encounter relationship with Jesus Christ in new and vibrant ways through the vehicle that He established on this earth before ascending to heaven. We have access to the same foundation and power as the first-century church, and from the lessons we learn in the Acts 2 process and the empowerment of the Holy Spirit, we will find our hope again.

# 5 EMPOWERED

A healthy church is God's idea. Jesus is the head and builder of the church, and He didn't make a mistake in how He built it. We have a blueprint of what He did in the form of the vital, growing church of Acts 2, which was born through prayer and with the Spirit as power.

If you ask a variety of people across denominational lines the purpose of the Holy Spirit in the church, you'll get a wide range of answers. I believe the strongest doctrinal case for the purpose of Spirit-empowerment is in carrying out the transformative mission of God among both the un-churched people and the stagnant, uninspired believers. With the challenges facing the church today, we can't rely on our own ingenuity, intellect, and human effort. God hasn't abandoned us to that fruitless recourse, but when we take hold of the Spirit as power, He fully equips and emboldens us to present hope to a lost world.

The Holy Spirit helps us to be more than we are. He empowers us, and the same Spirit that rested on a murderer, turning him into a deliverer; on a shepherd boy, turning him into a king; and on a long-haired womanizer, turning him into a judge, does not momentarily "rest" upon us. The Holy Spirit stayed with fishermen and turned them into disciples. He converted a religious murderer, indwelled him, and enabled him to write much of the New Testament. And most notably, the Spirit lived in and through a carpenter who is the Savior of the world. The Spirit empowers every believer who accepts His saving grace and humbly makes himself available to be used by God.

The Holy Spirit will also help you say more than you know. Most obviously, those who received the Holy Spirit in Acts 2 began speaking with other tongues as the Spirit gave them utterance. This word "utterance" is the Greek *apophthengomai,* which means "Spirit-inspired speech" and which can empower words in our normal language as surely as speaking in tongues.

Emboldened by the Holy Spirit, Peter may be the best example of this. Right after the Spirit fell in the upper room, he stood up from among the eleven disciples, raised his voice, and addressed the crowd in a Spirit-inspired speech. The results were nothing short of miraculous; they baptized and added 3,000 people to the church that day.

The Holy Spirit helped Peter beyond his natural ability, and the listeners went from wondering why the believers were speaking in other tongues to asking, "What should we do?" to receive Christ. That same inspiration and empowerment are what enable us to share the gospel effectively.

The Holy Spirit also helps us do more than we can. Before commissioning us to share the gospel, Jesus promised us power. He said, "But you shall receive power when the Holy Spirit has come upon you; and you shall be witnesses to Me in Jerusalem, and in all Judea and Samaria, and to the end of the earth" (Acts 1:8).

The Spirit's power is the fulfillment of Jesus' promise that those who believe in Him would do the same works He did—and even greater.

Examples of God's power encourage us to believe the supernatural. After the Holy Spirit fell, the disciples performed many miracles, including, but not limited to, healing the sick, casting out demons, and discipling untold thousands. And unlike Spirit-touched heroes of the Old Testament who momentarily enjoyed His power, the believers in the Acts 2 church experienced the lingering, indwelling power of the Holy Spirit.

> The Spirit's power is the fulfillment of Jesus' promise that those who believe in Him would do the same works He did—and even greater.

## BUILDING ON A FIRST-CENTURY BLUEPRINT

The first-century church was founded in prayer. In Acts 1, we read that Jesus' church-development, core team consisted of Peter, James, John (the big three), the rest of the remaining disciples, His mother and brothers, and several women who helped support His earthly ministry. They all joined together in prayer.

The results of this prayer and founding blueprint were nothing short of miraculous. Imagine these things being true in each of our churches: This first-century church believers received the Holy Spirit willingly, demonstrated power supernaturally, were led effectively, prayed fervently, fellowshipped regularly, taught sound doctrine consistently, preached the gospel passionately, shared resources liberally, and *grew exponentially*. This last result was a consequence of all those factors that preceded it, perhaps, most notably, the empowerment those in the upper room first received when the Holy Spirit came upon them at Pentecost, the first event recorded in Acts 2.

The entire book of Acts is an account of the birth and growth of the first-century church. It recounts how Holy Spirit-empowered small groups of believers were devoted to the apostles in their teaching, fellowship, sharing of meals (including the Lord's Supper), prayer, and living out the Great Commission Jesus gave in some of His last earthly words. A global movement resulted that took the gospel story around the known world and one that endures today.

Jesus' command to go into all the world and preach the gospel was the vision at the forefront, and Peter voiced their objective: He said, "Repent and be baptized, every one of you, in the name of Jesus Christ for the forgiveness of your sins. And you will receive the gift of the Holy Spirit. The promise is for you and your children and for all who are far off—for all whom the Lord our God will call" (Acts 2:38–39 NIV).

We read that they had a sense of awe as they saw the Spirit move on the disciples, enabling them to perform miraculous signs and wonders. (And if you don't think that sharing their property, possessions, and finances with those in need was a miracle, you try it!) Their days consisted of worshipping together, sharing meals with great joy and generosity, praising God, and enjoying the goodwill of their community.

And as they lived out this organic, Spirit-empowered life, God exploded their numbers.

## WHAT SPIRIT-EMPOWERMENT IS AND IS NOT

Experiencing Spirit-empowered discipleship means understanding that our relationship goes beyond mere belief or the washing away of sins. (These are the means through which Christ makes a relationship possible, but a life of following Him and knowing Him intimately yet awaits.) It isn't about doing more for God, performing at a higher level, or even experiencing signs and wonders.

It's about knowing God. In Jesus' great prayer, He explained, "And this is eternal life, that they may know You, the only true God, and Jesus Christ whom You have sent" (John 17:3). Paul perfectly understood this goal and privilege. To the believers in Philippi, he related that no power, prestige, or wealth could compete with the thrill of knowing God. Compared to the wonder and joy of his relationship with God, he explained that everything else is only "rubbish." He wrote,

> But what things were gain to me, these I have counted loss for Christ. Yet indeed I also count all things loss for the excellence of the knowledge of Christ Jesus my Lord, for whom I have suffered the loss of all things, and count them as rubbish, that I may gain Christ and be found in Him, not having my own righteousness, which is from the law, but that which is through faith in Christ, the righteousness which is from God by faith; that I may know Him and the power of His resurrection, and the fellowship of His sufferings, being conformed to His death. (Phil. 3:7–10)

Every spiritual discipline, every behavioral truth, every spiritual activity rings hollow without a growing relationship with Christ—and will eventually bring frustration, disappointment, or burnout. We

**We can't expect to operate in our own strength in order to accomplish God's work on the earth.**

can't expect to operate in our own strength in order to accomplish God's work on the earth. All of our good motivations, our pumped-up willpower, and our carefully crafted habits are insufficient. Learning and doing, apart from a growing relationship with God, will only tend to enlarge our pride—or crush us with disappointment.

When we're Spirit-empowered, every act of service and devotion, every discipline, every behavior is a byproduct of our relationship with Christ and reflects His work within us made possible through His Holy Spirit.

In the Old Testament, they made a house for the Lord, and His presence filled the Holy of Holies. To enter meant being exposed to so much of His holy presence that it was death to anyone but the high priest. In short, the God of the Old Testament was not a God to touch.

That has all changed, for the Spirit came upon flesh, filling us; God no longer only occupies buildings and doesn't need to rest on select people, temporarily or intermittently. He indwells us in a relationship of great intimacy and depth, something far beyond the moments of temporary Spirit-empowerment described in the Old Testament. God now engages those who follow Him in a relationship that gives the necessary context for every subsequent step of belief and behavior, knowing and doing.

Because He is in us and we are in Him, we want to know Him more and serve Him with our whole hearts—and then experience it. This is true transformation!

## REAL TRANSFORMATION

Transformation occurs at both a personal level and a corporate one. Though our Western mindset tends to focus on the individual, without whom there would be no group, a few people being transformed with the empowerment of the Holy Spirit are simply  not enough to carry out the Great Commission by themselves. Corporate, congregational transformation and Spirit-empowerment are necessary to ensure that our churches, regardless of size, are healthy and experiencing relationship with Christ.

Congregational transformation is more than the process of changing beliefs and behaviors, more than just changing goals, technologies, or systems, and more than examining our present condition and asking the right questions. Transformation is the necessary work of the Spirit that creates these processes and forms relationship at a corporate level—and it is this relationship that engenders lasting change or ushers in revival.

Transformation is a biblical concept found throughout the Word. It's rooted in the principles of spiritual renewal and formation into the image of Christ. It's also the favorite concept the apostle Paul used to describe the radical change involved in salvation and the work of the Holy Spirit in believers' lives.

Transformation is the result of the empowering work of the Holy Spirit. More knowledge and better behaviors can be the (temporary) results of hard work and personal initiative, but transformation happens only when the Spirit fosters an intimate relationship between the believer and the Lord.

At the center of the Acts 2 Journey is the belief that congregational-level transformation is still possible. Everywhere we turn, we find leaders who want their churches to grow and thrive. When I see their hearts and visions for the future, I know the church's best years are still ahead. Often, it seems, we can believe that miracles, promises, and the power of God occurred for people in the Bible, in the historical past, or on distant mission fields, but they aren't true for us personally or for the modern

Western church. But if the Bible, history, and reports of miracles abroad do anything, they should encourage us to see that if it has happened before, God can do it again, for nothing is impossible with Him!

Transformation begins in the hearts of the people—in the hearts of the congregants. It begins internally within individuals' hearts and minds and spreads as they are discipled, they disciple others in turn, and they share with others through Spirit-inspired speech. It begins as they *connect, grow, serve, go,* and *worship.* It begins as an internal process that combines knowledge, behavior, and relationship in order to transition a believer forward into a new or revitalized life in the Spirit.

Transformation is possible for any congregation, but it doesn't happen overnight. It's a process, not an event. It's a journey, not a destination. Just as the metamorphic transformation that Paul speaks of renews hearts and minds over time, congregational transformation isn't an instant result pressed upon people; it's a journey that begins from within and is only possible over time.

A revitalized church is one that pursues and obeys God passionately, and the revitalization process we see before us has its genesis in the functions Luke wrote about: fellowship, discipleship, gift-oriented ministry, evangelism, and worship. A healthy church is one that . . .

- Engages and maintains loving relationships (*connect*)
- Develops and mobilizes the people (*grow*)
- Acts with clear direction and outward focus (*serve*)
- Reproduces and multiplies His mission in other peoples and places (*go*)
- Pursues and obeys God passionately (*worship*)

These functions impact how we encounter God and each other as individuals, but they're just elements of another program without the anointing of the Holy Spirit.

Since the turn of the century, Pentecostalism has been a leader in world evangelism and discipleship. The growth rate for the Renewal Movement from 1910 to 2010 was nearly four times the prior growth rate of both Christianity as a whole and the world's population. From 2010 to 2025, the growth rate is expected to be twice as fast for both. Many churches are vibrant, healthy, and growing, and virtually every leader is eager to learn how to have the greatest possible impact for the kingdom of God. No matter how large or small a church may be, we face a daunting task: winning the unreached and under-churched people of the world. We desperately need divine empowerment. We need extra ability beyond our own capability. We need churches that are united, free of dissension, biblically designed, and Spirit-anointed.

> We need churches that are united, free of dissension, biblically designed, and Spirit-anointed.

We need to become like the church in Acts 2.

## THE UNFINISHED TASK

I became a pastor without even one day of pastoral ministry experience. Everything I knew about ministry was from being an evangelist. Though First Assembly of God in North Little Rock, Arkansas, probably received a hundred resumes, each with more pastoral experience than I had, for some reason, they chose me.

I was thirty-nine-years-old. I had never baptized anyone, dedicated a baby, or done any of the dozens of ministry tasks even a young pastor has done many times. However, God kept me at First Assembly for fifteen years and blessed the church. Why? I believe it was because of the transformation that occurred. We were on a journey of Spirit-empowered change, and this—more than experience and familiarity with beliefs and behaviors—created a relationship dynamic that changed people's lives.

I don't say this to pat myself on the back—quite the contrary. I share it to reveal that I felt completely unqualified for the task. But because the Holy Spirit had carte blanche in that congregation, transformation was possible—and that enabled me to carry out God's work there despite my lack of experience. I was committed, and God began to grow and develop what has become the Acts 2 process, because I wasn't content for us to stay where we were.

You may be reading this and thinking that the task before you—not just the fulfillment of the Great Commission but seeing revitalization in your church—is intimidating, discouraging, and humanly impossible. Satan may be insinuating that transformation is impossible, that the downward slide is inexorable, and that defeat for the church on earth is already spelled out in prophecy.

You may have lost hope.

You may feel under-qualified, insufficient, and underpowered for the task God has ahead of you and your congregation. You may feel locked into the "mom and pop" model where you are doing the entire ministry—and burning yourself out.

I would argue that if this is the case, you're in exactly the right place. We must recognize that we don't possess the power, ingenuity, and ability to pull this off. Only the transformative power of the Holy Spirit will allow us to rekindle the passion for evangelism and mission, change the climate of the church, and disciple a priesthood of believers within the church.

I believe the process God instituted in Acts 2 provides us with the blueprint necessary to remodel how we do ministry, turn the tide, stay relevant with current and future generations, and carry out the task Jesus gave us before His ascension.

I've mentioned before that I lacked the process and that what God showed me in Acts 2 provided the strategy, but the best strategy only works when we simultaneously embrace the power of the Holy Spirit.

We must never forget that the supernatural power of God was the defining element in the first-century church; it ushered in revival at various points in history, and it continues to transform lives and congregations to this day.

I've never felt qualified when entering any position I've held in ministry, and perhaps none of us are qualified to usher revitalization into the church. That simply means we all have a strong incentive to be totally dependent on God and the leading and power of the Holy Spirit. Truly, we can do nothing apart from Him—but with God, all things are possible.

There is hope.

# UNIT II
# FINDING HIS HEART

# 6 CREATING SPIRIT-EMPOWERED DISCIPLES

The Holy Spirit's power is vital to an effective leader and a vibrant church. While Spirit-empowered churches are our goal, we must recognize that churches aren't made up of bricks and mortar but are made up of a far more valuable asset than real estate: people.

The first and most basic building blocks of any church are *people*. At the core of the Acts 2 process is having Spirit-empowered disciples who are encountering Jesus, experiencing the fullness of the Holy Spirit, learning Scripture, and engaging with God's people. In fact, the primary objective of the entire Acts 2 process is to see unbelievers transformed into fully developed followers of Christ who are able to reproduce believers.

If we make disciples, the natural result is a strong, robust community of faith; but if we simply try to add warm bodies, we will rarely get disciples. Spirit-empowered discipleship is utterly vital.

This again is where we encounter the importance of relational or experiential truth. Learning and doing (education and effort) without encountering the Holy Spirit are counter-productive—in fact, it's dry, lifeless, and destined for failure.

Our churches don't need nice, cookie-cutter Christians; they need Spirit-empowered priests.

## SOUND DOCTRINE AND DISCIPLESHIP

Undeniably, sound doctrine is foundational to the strength and effectiveness of the church, and it's impossible to have sound disciples without sound doctrine. The truth of God shapes and molds the people of God for life and service.

While many churches are satisfied with their discipleship process, alarming research statistics indicate that many churches have discipleship deficiencies, that upcoming generations are leaving the faith at an alarming rate, and that professing Christians know less and less about the content of the Bible. The results are frightening.

Dave Kinnaman, president of the Barna Group, states, "In virtually every study we conduct, representing thousands of interviews every year, born-again Christians fail to display much attitudinal or behavioral evidence of transformed lives."[2]

Seminary president Dr. Albert Mohler writes on his website, "Christians who lack biblical knowledge are the products of churches that marginalize biblical knowledge. Bible teaching now often accounts for only a diminishing fraction of the local congregation's time and attention."[3]

Many of our churches have abandoned Sunday school as a means of discipleship but aren't offering a replacement for systematic study of God's Word. In short, our ability to create Spirit-empowered disciples hinges on our ability to disciple, period.

Just as with the Great Commission, this is an impossible task in our own strength and ingenuity. So if we aren't being reinvigorated and empowered for our tasks by the Holy Spirit, we won't be able to create an environment for upcoming generations to experience the power and presence of the Lord in a way that also teaches them sound doctrine.

But we don't need a few more programs. We need disciples experiencing the Spirit's power.

What do we need to do in order to accomplish this task of discipleship? Well, Jesus told His disciples to "wait."

Are we still waiting?

## WAIT

It's interesting to note that one of Jesus' last words wasn't "go" but "wait." What were His disciples waiting for?

He had no intention for them to begin fulfilling the Great Commission without the power to accomplish the task. He said, "Wait in the city . . ." (Luke 24:49) and "You will be baptized with the Holy Spirit not many days from now" (Acts 1:5). Jesus knew they couldn't do it with their own inge-

> It appears that many people today have traded the Pentecostal experience for respectability.

nuity. They needed *immersion*. In Acts 1:8, we read the promise: "But you shall receive power."

Followers of Jesus need *Spirit-empowerment*.

It appears that many people today have traded the Pentecostal experience for respectability. Because we've seen some goofiness (from people who were goofy before they were filled with the Spirit), many have rejected the experience of encountering the power of the Holy Spirit. Sound teaching in the classroom is important, but it should never replace the prayer room and the revitalizing empowerment that comes from seeking God and His resource to us—His Holy Spirit.

Remember, what Jesus wants us to do is *impossible*. We aren't capable of loving our enemies, forgiving those who have wronged us, creating Spirit-empowered disciples, or walking a supernatural path to take the good news to every corner of the world on our own. We have severe capacity issues. We must believe powerful stories are still being written, and then we must write them in our churches, large and small—and the lives of Spirit-filled disciples are our letters.

In the previous chapter, I shared that I have never really felt ready for the tasks God has assigned to me. As we contemplate the tasks ahead of us, we must understand that God isn't waiting to equip us with more power in the moment of each task. No, if we have the Holy Spirit, we *already have all the power we need!*

## HE ISN'T OUR LAST RESORT

This may sound like subtle semantics, but stay with me—I believe Spirit-empowerment is more about "pre" than "post." Let me explain.

Skimming through the Old Testament reveals the people of God continually getting into desperate situations and calling out to Him—then the Red Sea splits, the ax head floats, a shepherd boy conquers a giant, manna appears, or some other miraculous occurrence rescues them.

We've reinforced a similar behavior with our disciples. We say, "God, when I run out of gas, exhaust all options, and can go no further, come rescue me." Yes, there are times when we need miracles, but think about this: If God wants us to build a church, change a life, restore a broken family, or reach an unreached people group, wouldn't it be easier if He just did it Himself? Or maybe He should let us try and try, and when we run out of steam, He could swoop down and perform the impossible.

He did exactly that many times before the day of Pentecost. Jesus could have launched His disciples with the guarantee that He would show up in unexpected moments and handle their challenging situations. Instead, He said they would receive power—the same power of the Spirit that Jesus claimed as His own power source—*before* they got into those situations. The Holy Spirit came upon them, His power indwelled them, and *that* is how they grew the church.

In the Old Testament, the anointing came upon individuals sporadically when they were depleted or desperate. Under the New Covenant, the anointing is available continually and in advance of the need, providing the necessary resource for every Spirit-empowered disciple of Christ. John tells us, "The Holy One has given you His Spirit" (John 2:20 NLT).

We already have Him. We don't have to operate in our own strength, stumble, fall, and ask for rescue. We can pray and proceed out of the Spirit's enablement to move forward under His guidance, direction, and empowerment to carry out God's tasks for us on the earth.

Spirit-empowerment should be our first thought, hope, and desire—not our last resort.

> Spirit-empowerment should be our first thought, hope, and desire—not our last resort.

## TRANSFORMED DISCIPLES

Earlier, we discussed the importance of the transformative work of the Holy Spirit. Let's revisit this again in the context of the Spirit-empowered disciple—specifically, one of a generation hungry for experience.

Spirit-empowered disciples don't experience an isolated event but a process of complete transformation. Paul describes this in his words, "And we all, with unveiled face, beholding the glory of the Lord, are being transformed into the same image from one degree of glory to another. For this comes from the Lord who is the Spirit" (2 Cor. 3:18 ESV).

We each progress through a spiritual journey. On this journey, we have a biblical directive to keep growing. To illustrate this pattern of growth, we have defined five classes of people who attend our churches each week:

- **Unbelievers**—People who haven't received Christ as Lord and Savior of their lives.

- **Believers**—People who've received Christ as Lord (belief system) but haven't yet become learners who obey God's Word (behavior).

- **Disciples**—People who adhere to the teachings and practices of growing in Christ and demonstrate a lifestyle corresponding to God's Word.

- **Servant-Leaders**—People who've grown in the direction, ways, and timing of the Lord and share their knowledge of Christ with others so they, too, can learn His direction, ways, and timing. They're involved in different aspects of church life (bus drivers, altar workers, greeters, deacons, Sunday school teachers, etc.).

- **Reproducers**—People who mentor others through relationship to the point where they become servant-leaders.

The goal is for each believer to continually grow and mature, going from glory to glory. The classic example of this process is the life of Peter—the disciple who had such incredible highs and lows. Peter recognized Jesus as the Messiah, but moments later Jesus rebuked him for speaking for Satan. Peter is infamous as the disciple who stepped out of the boat and then sank when he took his eyes off Jesus and as the one who spoke so bravely about never leaving Jesus' side but then ran off and later denied Jesus three times.

This same man, who couldn't find his voice in front of a servant girl, found *apophthengomai*—Spirit-inspired speech that empowered him to speak to thousands after Pentecost. He's also the same man who hypocritically associated with Judaizers, neglecting the Gentile believers, after being the one who saw the vision of a sheet let down from heaven, which paved the way for the gospel to go to Gentiles. He's the same man who wrote 1 Peter and 2 Peter and who, according to tradition, is the first head of the church on earth. Peter knew the source of true spiritual life: the gospel of grace. In his second letter, he described a process of spiritual growth from virtuous choices to authentic love and then explained:

> For if these things are yours and abound, you will be neither barren nor unfruitful in the knowledge of our Lord Jesus Christ. For he who lacks these things is short-sighted, even to blindness, and has forgotten that he was cleansed from his old sins. Therefore, brethren, be even more diligent to make your call and election sure, for if you do these things you will never stumble; for so an entrance will be supplied to you abundantly into the everlasting kingdom of our Lord and Savior Jesus Christ. (2 Peter 1:8–11)

This surely is the testimony of a man whose life as a believer wasn't a one-time event but a transformation process over time. He was never the same after Pentecost, nor was he a finished product—which should give all of us hope.

Like the process of spiritual growth Peter described, we're all in a state of *becoming*—none of us has arrived. We're discipleship works in progress.

## WE HAVE WHAT THEY WANT

This generation is hungry for experiences, which is evidenced by their fascination with the paranormal, superhuman, and mystical. People hungry for heroes and powers greater than themselves have flocked to movies like *Spider-Man*, *Superman*, *The Lord of the Rings*, *The Avengers*, *Twilight Saga*, and even *Star Wars*. (That last one has a sequel coming out in December.)

A generation hungry for experiencing something beyond the natural is looking for power and is preoccupied with the paranormal. From the brooding teen vampires of the *Twilight Saga* to the curious adolescent wizards in *Harry Potter*, stories of characters with extraordinary powers abound. Audiences may recognize the mythical nature of the stories, but they're entertained and inspired by heroes who rise above the masses and the challenges of a shifting, uncertain world.

All of the myths point to a fantastic story that's absolutely true: A great King has come to rescue His people. A great conflict threatens us all, but the King is the ultimate hero who sacrificed Himself for us. Thankfully, our story isn't a made-up myth. It's completely, absolutely, and wonderfully true! I believe this generation understands an underlying life truth—there's a reality beyond the material world and a greater power is at work in this universe.

They are ripe for a transformative experience.

We should see ourselves as privileged to live in this time. Beyond gleaning symbolic truth from mythical characters, as followers of Christ we can experience a real presence and power beyond human capacity. We can be Spirit-empowered.

What this generation desires, we possess—and can experience on a daily basis. And even more, through Spirit-empowered discipleship, we can impart this same transformative experience to a hungry generation!

Church leaders talk about how to reach Millennials (those born after 1980) and many are making church experiences seeker-friendly. I believe the key to staying relevant is not just changing up our worship services but also creating an environment where they can experience the power of the Holy Spirit.

We're all looking for better answers; however, it isn't better answers we need but better *questions*. Our questions have focused on us—the people inside the church. The better questions are about them—the people outside our churches with whom we should be building relationships. The right questions will focus on them, and those better questions will give us the answers we need.

We must ask ourselves how well we're demonstrating this experience and how well we're participating in it. We have what this generation is hungry for, but do they even know we have it? Are we so busy being seeker-friendly that we're afraid to talk about the Holy Spirit when He should be our calling card with a generation that's hungry to experience His power?

## LIVE DEAD

We can't build disciples in our churches until we first experience this empowerment of the Spirit ourselves and demonstrate it to a hungry world. Passionate leaders are living Christ's call to the church quite vibrantly throughout the body of Christ, and lives are changing.

One of these cutting-edge ministries is the Live Dead movement where young people are committing their lives to God so radically that they strongly desire to go to the hardest mission fields—places where they could be persecuted and even killed. Young, empowered disciples are signing up by the hundreds to sell out to God, give everything they've got to abide with Christ, reach the unreached, and abandon anything that holds them back. They're learning that we'll obey the Lord Jesus and His commission as we return to the simplicity of abiding with Him, advance together to plant a church where the church doesn't exist, and embrace suffering and persecution for Jesus' sake as our normal reality.

These young men and women are hungry for an authentic connection with the Holy Spirit. They aren't seeking something easy, and they don't want to be preoccupied with materialism. They want to experience the reality of the gospel lived out in the most hostile parts of the world. As of this writing, it hasn't happened though they're willing to die for this—to Live Dead.

A member of the Live Dead team in North Africa writes:

When our missionaries are imprisoned or killed, we will send more missionaries. When our missionaries fail and our teams implode, we will repent, revise our structure, improve our preparation, training, and pastoral care, and send new teams.

Neither spiritual nor physical attacks will deter us from living among resistant people and lovingly proclaiming the gospel to them in Jesus' name.

We will not retreat!

People who are on fire for God let the Holy Spirit take the limits off what they think God can do. They're ready for anything, including dying for what they believe.

What would happen if our churches had this kind of Spirit-inspired passion? What would happen in your town or city if the people in your church were willing to live as ones who are dead to reach the hurting and lost?

It will never happen with emotionally fanned messages or programs or initiatives, and it's too much to do by ourselves. However, it can happen when the Holy Spirit fans our spirits into flame, because God is ready to empower disciples of Christ all across our hurting world.

# 7 ASSESSMENT

Experiencing the Holy Spirit's power is just as necessary as a strategic plan and process. Plans identify goals and direction. However, if you don't know where you are, you don't know how to get to your destination.

The Spirit-empowered, relational framework I've been describing proposes a transforming journey for all ages and stages of spiritual congregational development. The Holy Spirit will lead us in a relational journey with God's Son, God's Word, God's Spirit, and God's people. After you read the book and understand the full scope of the Acts 2 Journey, consider conducting an assessment of your church. You'll find instructions in this chapter, and an assessment tool is included on our website: acts2journey.com

If an Acts 2-modeled, Spirit-empowered, transformative congregation is the goal, we must ask ourselves what we are experiencing in our churches. If it is anything less than this, what must change? You must be honest with yourself about your current spiritual realities.

God's will is for His church to be healthy and to accomplish His mission. The road to a healthy church, regardless of size or age demographics, begins with asking the right questions of ourselves and assessing our current status as Spirit-empowered disciples.

Are we healthy? Can we even agree on the definition of a "healthy church"? Perhaps even more fundamentally, do we have the courage to assess ourselves honestly? We must look at what has happened in our congregations in the last three years and recognize that this is a likely predictor of what will happen in the next three years.

If we want to change our results, God must change our hearts. Then, with His guidance, we must change our direction, our relationships, and our activities. A rigorous, honest assessment is the starting point. If what we're doing isn't working, we must question it. If we aren't experiencing the Spirit's power, we must eagerly seek revitalization for ourselves as well as our churches.

Part of the Acts 2 process is using assessment tools designed to help churches determine their current condition and then prescribe a path to health, but these tools will do nothing for us if we don't have the courage to be honest and then act on our findings.

Every church should be asking the following questions:

1. Why do we exist? (Mission)
2. Where are we going? (Vision)
3. How should we behave? (Values)
4. How will we get there? (Strategic plan)
5. How will we engage new people? (Evangelize / Go)
6. How will we great them when they arrive? (Connect)
7. How will we disciple them? (Grow)
8. How will we train them to serve? (Serve)
9. How will we inspire them to be missional? (Go)
10. How will we help them encounter God? (Worship)

A question that is very difficult, but necessary is: Are we the right leaders for this time and place? Do we have a divine call to this church? Is the church our client, or is God our client? We must question ourselves and ask who we're trying to please—people or God. And, critically, if we are pastoring churches that have plateaued or are declining, we must decide if we're willing to seek help.

The future success of our churches and the corporate church hinges on our answers to these questions and many others. Our willingness to be honest and unreserved in answering these assessment questions will go a long way towards determining the types of answers we get and whether or not they are helpful.

## CONGREGATIONAL ASSESSMENT

I have asked some pretty pointed questions about the current state of your church. Understand something very important—determining the current reality of the church is not meant to discourage or depress anyone to the point of giving up. My goal is to inspire hope. Remember, it is God's church and Jesus is the builder. No matter the present situation or the current reality, transformation is possible.

To adopt the Acts 2 model, the first thing a church must do is determine their current reality. When a church engages in this process, they first must evaluate their position on a congregational life cycle to assess if vision, relationships, programs, and management are in proper alignment. As a church ages and becomes less missional, programs and management become more predominate than vision and relationships.

# Life Cycle Stages of a Church

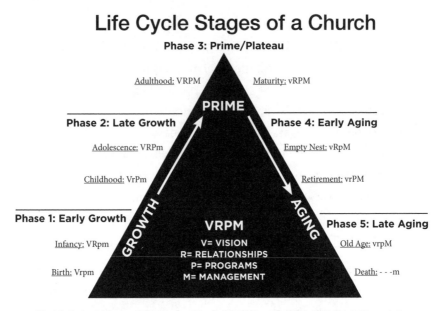

"The Life Cycle and Stages of Congregational Development," George Bullard Jr, 2001. Used with permission.

Once the church reaches maturity, if there is not intentional and continuous vision casting, relationship building, and ministry growth, the church tends to move from the ascending side of the life cycle to the descending side.

No matter at what stage a church is in their life cycle, there is always hope. When a church finds itself at the apex of the life cycle or on the descending side where the current vision is weak or nonexistent, we believe that through the power of the Holy Spirit, it is possible to define a compelling, spiritually sought-after vision for greater hope, ministry, and growth.

"Transformation is not a destination. For congregations it is not a place of arrival where the transformation journey can be declared as over. It is an ongoing journey. Congregations do not transform once. They are continually transforming. Congregations who continually transform hardwire into their culture the process of always engaging in transition and change."[4] When I began leading pastors, God inspired me to equip and encourage them and their churches in a specific way. We developed a survey for our pastors, and we identified eight needs they had. I built a curriculum to address those eight needs. Every month, I would have a teaching day, and I and other presenters would address one of those needs. We went through the year and then repeated the cycle so as many pastors as possible could participate.

On our website, acts2journey.com, you'll find a list of tools, assessments, and other resources. There you can download the congregational assessment. It only takes a few minutes to fill out. You'll discover which of the five functions your church does well and which need some attention.

The congregational assessment will help you "take the temperature" of your leaders, and perhaps, each team of leaders in your church. With the information you derive, you and your leaders will be able to form strategic plans based on solid feedback, not just guesses about the church's needs and goals. Ask people to be completely honest in their responses.

## THE FUNCTIONS AREN'T MULTIPLE CHOICE

Measuring your current realities in conjunction with the five functions derived from Acts 2:42–47 is your starting point in expanding your kingdom potential. We ask every church that goes through the Acts 2 Journey which of the five functions— *connect, grow, serve, go,* or *worship*—they think is their greatest strength. Almost every church says they are strongest in worship or *connect* (fellowship), and almost everyone lists *go* (evangelism) as their weakest function.

One particular church's response to this question was telling because it exposed the need for honest assessment. When asked this question, the ten or twelve older adults on the pastor's dream team said that worship was their strongest function. When asked why, they said, "Oh, our worship music is just wonderful! Everybody just feels the presence of the Lord. It's amazing!"

However, the young couple in the group both firmly shook their heads "no." It was obvious they shared a different view from the older people on the team. Everyone looked at them, and it was an embarrassing moment, but they needed to recognize the disconnection. The young couple was the youth leadership team, and they pointed out that the older saints loved worship hymns but these songs weren't resonating with the younger people in the church.

Over the course of a year, this church worked hard to figure out a strategy for getting where they wanted to be, but it could only start when they honestly assessed where they were.

An older gentleman from another church began the Acts 2 Journey with his arms firmly crossed. He seemed to be there against his will. However, during the assessment, he began to break down and weep as he saw the results that would play out should they continue in the direction they were taking. This same man ultimately became a leader for their entire effort to ask "better" questions.

Their questions had all been about "us"—the people already at the church. The better questions were about "them"—the people they wanted to bring into their church.

When they stopped asking the wrong questions, they started getting the right answers.

Near the end of their effort to affect changes, they made a video featuring this older leader, who had been in the church for at least thirty years. The video showed him standing at the fork of a gravel road. In the video, he said it was time for the church to take a new path. He asked everyone to follow him, and that was how this church introduced a new vision and direction for their congregation.

It was time for them to get healthy, but they first had to ask the right questions and make an honest assessment. Without these hard questions and perhaps harder answers, they were never going to make the necessary changes.

That same choice is before each of us: Will we be willing to face the truth and do what is necessary to bring change to our church?

## ASSUMPTIONS

We have some important considerations when gauging the health of a church, large or small. The first of these is whether the size of a church is the most telling indicator of health. While logic says a healthy church will be growing numerically, it's also true that disciples may be growing spiritually in a church that isn't increasing in attendance. We have a tendency to think that "bigger is better." The fact is that small congregations *can* be healthy, missional, and effective in making a difference in their communities. They may sometimes be the only church body impacting those communities.

The truth is that bigger just means larger. A church isn't necessarily better or more effective simply because it's larger. Our desire is to have healthy, vibrant churches of every size that are being revitalized by the power of the Holy Spirit.

You're reading this book because you want to be a better leader and you want your church to grow—in depth and in size. It's best, however, to focus on creating a healthy environment, a hothouse where people can grow in their love for God, for each other, and for people outside the church. If you create a healthy environment and trust God for the growth, it will come.

# 8 MISSION

----------------------------------------

The Acts 2 church process begins with understanding the mission of the church. The New Testament church's mission is timeless. It's the same today as it was the day Christ ascended, and it's the same for each and every church. In the context of our process, we use the term *mission* as the objective from God to the New Testament church.

Our mission, which we call the Great Commission, was established with Christ's words on the Mount of Ascension: "Therefore go and make disciples of all nations, baptizing them in the name of the Father and of the Son and of the Holy Spirit, and teaching them to obey everything I have commanded you. And surely I am with you always, to the very end of the age" (Matt. 28:19–20 NIV).

The Great Commission focuses on the belief system Christ taught, and it establishes the purpose for the church's existence. We are commissioned to worship the Lord with all we have, to win the lost, to train believers to become disciples, to use our ministry gifts, and to find environments of fellowship for connection.

What we often call the Great Commandment serves as a guide for our beliefs—our attitudes and actions—*how* we go about this Great Commission. Jesus spelled out the Great Commandment, and love was front and center: "'Love the Lord your God with all your heart and with all your soul and with all your mind.' This is the first and greatest commandment. And the second is like it: 'Love your neighbor as yourself'" (Matt. 22:37–39 NIV).

In the light of our mission to make disciples, we can sometimes neglect that *love* is the guiding force that should govern how we pursue our mission. Paul admonishes us that without love, evidence of Spirit-empowerment—such as speaking in tongues, prophecy, and faith to move mountains—is hollow and nothing but a clanging cymbal, profiting us nothing.

It's as vital to have love guiding our mission as it is to have the Holy Spirit empowering us to complete it.

The mission of the church continues through each of us. As leaders, it's our responsibility to disciple the people who can bring this message to those who are searching for truth and looking for hope.

> It's as vital to have love guiding our mission as it is to have the Holy Spirit empowering us to complete it.

My friend Denny Miller has written extensively about the Holy Spirit and the mission of God. In his book, *The Spirit of God in Missions*, he writes, "The church faces a great challenge. More than two thousand years ago, Jesus commissioned His church to take the gospel to every nation and people on earth. Today, as never before, that goal is within reach. Missiologists today talk of closure, or completing Christ's commission."[5]

How could that happen? Is it possible? It is possible, but only with God's enabling. Let's believe in fresh renewal and empowerment to accomplish our mission.

## A PEOPLE OF MISSION

When considering any passage of Scripture, we must look at the rational meaning and extract behavioral applications from the text, but we also need to look deeper into the passage. We must always ask ourselves this question: What is revealed in the text about the character, person, and heart of God? We must then allow the Spirit to lead us into a heartfelt response. This relational perspective is critical to developing a more intimate relationship with the One who is Truth.

It all comes back to relationship—one of the most important elements that separates Christianity from religions that are all about human efforts to reach God. Everything stems from or is initiated by a relationship with Christ through the Holy Spirit. It all starts with knowing Him and engaging the personal relationship He offers through faith in Christ's sacrifice.

We can too easily be distracted by "doing good things for God" instead of knowing Him and serving Him out of an over-flowing heart. People may engage in disciplines and exert effort to fulfill the commands of Scripture, but those who engage in a lot of spiritual activity without a growing relationship with Christ will be frustrated and disappointed—eventually, they'll burn out. When we operate in our own strength, we soon find our motivations, willpower, and habits to be insufficient. The longer we appear to pull it off without trusting in God's purpose and power, the more our pride grows.

For the Spirit-empowered disciple, knowledge and acts of service are the products of a relationship with Christ. They reflect His work within us rather than being goals in and of themselves.

## MAKE THE MISSION HUMAN

Love is how we carry out the mission, but relationship is what makes the mission *human*—giving it flesh and bone, faces and personalities. When the people walking through a church's doors are its most valuable commodity, an attitude of "nickels and noses" won't cut it. Those people will only feel a call toward discipleship as they are embraced in relationship and promoted in their own relationships with Christ Jesus.

For many people, those relationships require a sense of ownership—they have to be invested in order to feel they're a part of things. When I was at First Assembly of God in Little Rock, we were going through a building process. Curiously, it wasn't the architect who made one of the most interesting contributions to the design phase of the project.

We lived in the parsonage the first two years at First Assembly, and a congregant named Verl Simpson lived next door to us. Our houses were conveniently located across the street from the church but in an interesting part of town. Up the road one way was Memorial Hospital, and two blocks away was the VA Hospital. The VA Hospital had a unit for people with mental challenges, and sometimes, those people would wander the neighborhood when they got out, knocking on doors and asking for money. Verl Simpson nominated himself as the protector for my wife and daughter, particularly if I wasn't there.

An early riser, Verl was always urging me to get up earlier—never mind that he had to take a nap at 11 a.m.! We would banter good-naturedly about it, and I (a notorious night owl) teased him that if I wanted to sleep my day away, I would get up as early as he did.

One day he told my wife, Johanna, "That husband of yours is intent on moving this church, is he not?" He didn't wait for a response before telling her, "Well, I'm not going. Whoever he sells this church to, that's what I'm going to become. If it's to a Baptist church, I'm going to become a Baptist. If he sells it to Catholics, I'm going to become Catholic."

Verl wasn't the only dissenter; the church had been divided about what to do with this property for years before I even got there. So when it was nearly time to start construction, I knew I needed to get more people on board. I invited a group of people to the church for refreshments in order to show them samples of everything that would be in the new building. I had cuttings of the carpet, pew samples, and all the drawings up on the wall. The architect was present to answer questions and explain the drawings. I hoped that this would take away the fears and misgivings of the holdouts.

Well, Uncle Verl, as we called him, decided to show up. He had his hands stuffed deeply into his pockets and a scowl on his face. He just walked around looking at everything and not saying a word. I watched him out of the corner of my eye and wondered what he was thinking. I noticed that when he got to the structural drawings, he studied them for a long time.

After he got through studying the architect's drawings, he came over to me and asked, "Pastor, where's the architect? I've got a question for him."

I groaned inside but brought the architect over to talk with us. "I'm looking at the platform, right?" Verl asked. The architect confirmed that as correct, so Verl went on. "Well, it looks to me like you have the audio-visual in good shape, but I don't think you've drawn an adequate distribution for the airflow over the platform. My pastor deserves to be cool when he preaches."

The architect's eyebrows went up, but the two men took a closer look at the drawings. The architect finally said, "You know, Mr. Simpson, I believe you're right. I think that's an oversight we need to correct."

A massive smile broke out on Verl's face. His chest seemed to swell, and his attitude was completely different. He had made a contribution; he had challenged the man and won!

Verl was on my side the rest of the way, helping advocate for the new building he had "helped design." He and his wonderful wife even moved to be closer to the new church, and he continued to serve as an usher. We gave Verl Simpson all the credit for his contribution, and when we moved into the new building, I would frequently say that if it weren't for him, I would be sweating while I preached.

People make all the difference, and when they buy in and take ownership, you'll be amazed at what they can do! It may seem ridiculous to think that the success or failure of an endeavor can hinge on one person, but it definitely does hinge on individuals.

Can one person change everything? Well, a very unlikely person changed a small but key component of our new building, and his contribution helped keep me cool and collected while we pursued God's mission and vision for our church.

The church is composed of individuals, each one bearing Christ's assignment on the earth and each one capable of receiving His vision for their lives and for the lives they touch. Each one of us can make a difference as we show the world our vision for what a life connected to God can look like, carrying out His mission for the church.

## CAN JUST ONE PERSON MAKE A DIFFERENCE?

Can one person change *everything*?

I think we could say with confidence that Abraham Lincoln changed his world, from writing his Gettysburg Address, which inspired a nation, to seeing our country through a brutal civil war that helped abolish slavery. Winston Churchill saw England and the Allies through dark days and some of the worst moments in World War II and inspired free nations to continue to fight against the tyranny of Hitler's Germany. Certainly, the world would be different if Hitler had crossed the English Channel. We could probably all agree that Nelson Mandela, who spent twenty years in jail for his opposition to apartheid, helped bring healing to an entire country with his magnanimous attitude toward former enemies when he emerged from prison a matured man and became an influential president in South Africa. Mother Teresa's life of poverty and outreach to others was so powerful that it didn't just change the lives of the people in India but provided a platform for her compassion to change the lives of countless millions around the world.

One person *can* make a difference. The names I've listed are just a few heroes of humanity, but you don't have to be one of these paragons to make a difference.

Is it possible that even the young daughter of a drug addict could do the same?

## THE MASON JAR

Can one person really adopt the Great Commission and the Great Commandment?

Years ago, I was receiving a missions offering, and a six-year-old girl brought me a Mason fruit jar with $12.45 in it. She told me, "I've been saving money to buy my mommy a house, but I want to give it to you for these Bibles." Her mother was a drug addict, strung out on meth and facing twenty-three felony counts and three years in prison. The little girl had no idea that what she could save in a jar would never buy a house. All she knew was that something was broken in her home, and she was trying to help fix it.

I didn't want to take that money from the little girl, and I tried to give it back to her because I knew a bit about her situation.

I knew her grandfather, who was a pastor. Her mother, the pastor's daughter, had been raised in church, had attended Sunday school, and had been a regular at church camp. But she had lost her way and had become a dysfunctional individual. Her little daughter was present that night at her grandfather's church where I was speaking because the court had taken her children from her care and placed them with the grandparents. That's what I knew and why I couldn't bear to take the contents of her Mason jar.

She was so insistent and passionate, however, that I took that Mason jar and gave the money to buy Bibles for China. Her unselfish act of generosity was an inspiration to others. Later, I took her and her grandparents to a missions banquet where we were raising funds to buy more Bibles—and by telling her story, those present were moved to pledge more than $2 million for Bibles.

The power of one little girl's faith changed countless lives. She filled one Mason jar with $12.45, but it was a seed, like the widow's mite, in the hands of God. She was thinking of buying a house, but the Holy Spirit was thinking of restoring a home. She planted a seed, and it not only inspired millions of dollars for Bibles but produced fruit within her own family.

Miraculously, when her mother stood before the judge to face the consequences of her actions, she didn't receive what she expected. "You deserve no mercy," he told her. "Your parole officer says you're the worst case he's ever dealt with. You've lost your home, your husband, your job, your dignity, and your children— they've been taken away from you." He paused, considering, before saying something unexpected: "I don't know why I'm doing this . . . but I'm going to give you one more chance."

She went to a halfway house instead of prison, and the real harvest of that little girl's seed was that her mother was saved and delivered.

Ten years later, that mother is a worship leader in church and sings praises to the Lord nearly every week. They've had trouble, including relapses, but the power of one little girl's faith meant a world of difference to her mother and continues to inspire others every time I share her story.

We have a mission as a corporate church, but we can't fulfill it without *individuals*.

## THE POWER OF ONE

When we talk about the church, we think of a body of individuals who seek and serve the Lord together. We think of the power of "together" and what the Lord can do through a passionate leader and a group of Spirit-empowered believers.

While it's important for us to understand the power of "together," "together" can't occur if one person doesn't volunteer.

"Together" begins with just one person.

Talking about "one" makes me think of a song I used to preach against called "The Pied Piper." The song included the line, "One is the loneliest number." While the songwriters had it right that one person can be lonely and ineffectual, they weren't completely correct. You see, it only takes one person adopting the universal mission of the church to make an extraordinary difference. Throughout church history, God has used the vision, love, and courage of individuals to change the course of history. In many cases, these people appeared to be the most unlikely candidates for greatness, but they were humble enough to recognize two essential facts: their inadequacy and God's supreme adequacy. Trusting Him, they changed the world.

The revitalization of any church begins when even one person catches the dream of the Holy Spirit's empowerment to accomplish His mission on the earth. One person can't save the world, but one person with hope can start something else: revitalization.

# 9 VISION

Every church has the Great Commission as its mission; we don't get to vote on that. But each church needs a unique vision, which is how we fulfill the mission, and the vision of each church can be as individual as fingerprints or DNA. As important as it is for us to understand that every church shares the universal commission to go out and save the lost, it's also vital that we help define vision for the churches we lead.

*Vision* is often a misunderstood word, but for our purposes, a vision is our current understanding of God's preferred future for a person, group, or congregation. Stephen Covey defines it this way: "Vision is the best manifestation of creative imagination and the primary motivation of human action. It is the ability to see beyond our present reality, to create, to invent what does not yet exist, to become what we not yet are. It gives us capacity to live out our imagination instead of our memory."[6]

Vision is the ability to courageously explore possibilities. It understands who we are and what we're uniquely designed to do. It answers "Where are we going?" and "Why are we doing it?" and imagines life beyond present boundaries. It's based on truth, but it transcends current reality. It unites people, helps them focus on a destination, and dares them to push against the status quo.

Vision always involves risk and invites criticism, especially for the individuals into whom God breathes the dream that becomes a vision. Erwin McManus, pastor of Mosaic Church in Los Angeles, writes, "From the beginning, God has raised up men and women who have had the power of seeing. They understood the times in which they lived. They understood the context to which they were called. They had the ability to understand change and create change. They could both perceive and foresee."[7]

One of the primary problems in churches—especially those whose growth has become stunted—is the loss of vision. People forget why they are there. Often it isn't the pastor who has no vision; it's the people, who have lost track of their purpose as a church. Decline always follows, and it's the result of inward focus.

The church has a mission, but we also have a vision for what the world would look like reconnected to God. Our vision is our dream—that everyone would come to the saving knowledge of Christ and be restored to relationship with the Father. Our vision must be outward focused, thinking of "them" and not "us." Without this, we perish.

## SEEING WHAT ISN'T THERE

I've spoken with many church leaders who are afraid of the word *vision*, typically because they don't understand it or find the idea of setting a vision for a church intimidating. I frequently talk to leaders who tell me they aren't sure how to even find a vision, so I like to help demystify the process of describing a vision.

I try to simplify it for them by asking, "What would your church look like if God was in charge and could do whatever He wanted to do?" Some miss the point and say He's already in charge, but if we're truly honest, we can admit there are things in every church God would like to work on.

Vision, very simply, is the skill of seeing what isn't there.

How do we learn to do this? The only way to see what isn't there is through the eyes of the Spirit. Casting a vision for your church isn't about pulling visionary material out of yourself but about seeing what God is *already* dreaming for your church.

> Casting a vision for your church isn't about pulling visionary material out of yourself but about seeing what God is *already* dreaming for your church.

I'll give you a hint: God's dream for your church always involves people.

## SEE VISION BY LOOKING AT PEOPLE

A friend of mine was a perfect example of a pastor intimidated by setting a vision for his church. He had just been selected as the new pastor, and he found out that on his sixth Sunday—the day of his official installation as pastor—the message would be in three parts. A retired minister and longtime member of the congregation would share for ten minutes, talking about where the church had been. Then the superintendent would take ten minutes to describe what the church should be, and after that the new pastor would share his vision for the church's future.

Upon finding out the plan, my friend panicked—he didn't have a hint of a vision for the church. He had barely unpacked his belongings and had met only a few members of the congregation in the short time he had been there! He began to pray, and his prayers became more desperate as the big day approached.

On that day, my friend still had no idea what to share. The aged minister beautifully described the eight-decade history of the church, the superintendent masterfully explained the purpose and mission of the corporate church, and my friend walked up to the pulpit still clueless about what to say.

He stood there awkwardly for a few moments before suddenly catching sight of the smiling face of a seven-year-old girl he had met earlier, Amanda. He stepped down off the platform and walked to where she was sitting with her parents. Without really knowing what he was doing, he asked her to stand up and began to talk to her. He told her what he wanted to see happen in her life because she was a part of this church family. He said he wanted her to grow up to be a great woman of God, always know her church family loved her. He wanted her to feel she always belonged and someday meet the godly young man with whom she could spend the rest of her life there in that church. When he sat her back down, her mother and many others were wiping away tears.

My friend then had a young military man stand up and told him what he would find because he was part of the church. He said he hoped the young man would always feel welcome, would be a godly example, and that he and his fiancée would get married and see their dreams come to fruition there in that church. My friend spoke similarly to a young couple, then to a single mom and her children. He concluded by speaking to an elderly widower on the second row.

My friend later confessed that throughout all this, he didn't understand what was happening—until the aged minister was hugging him with tears in his eyes and the superintendent was vigorously shaking his hand and congratulating him on "the best *vision* I've ever heard."

Repeated over and over with each person was a similar refrain, which someone actually had to point out to my friend: "You said you wanted each of them to know that they belonged here. That's the only thing you repeated, and you said that to each of them."

Over the next few years, a clear vision for the church emerged: It would be a place of belonging where people could wrap their arms around anyone, connect with them, help them, and always make them feel welcome—no matter the choices they had made or the lives they had lived. It would be a place where "belonging is the beginning of believing and becoming," as they put it.

My friend learned that fateful Sunday that you can't find God's vision for your life or your church until you look at *people*. For you see, they are what God is looking at!

Vision isn't buildings, plans, or numbers. It isn't about programs or ministry tools.

Vision is about being the kind of people and the kind of church God wants us to be.

> Vision is about being the kind of people and the kind of church God wants us to be.

## THE AMANDA GAME

After telling this story, we like to play what we call the Amanda Game at our Acts 2 Journeys. We basically do what my friend did for Amanda; we ask a table full of leaders from a church to each take a turn speaking vision to a designated "Amanda" at the table. Each person in the room may take thirty seconds or a few minutes to share their hopes for their "Amanda's" future.

Of course, the real importance of the game isn't the exercise during the Journey but implementing it when they return to their churches. We give them an assignment: Play the Amanda Game in your heads at your churches. We urge them to let their thoughts begin to flow for people they don't even know and then gather the leadership team to share the results of the exercise.

We urge them not to limit this undercover vision-casting to Sundays at church but to make the exercise a chance to move their focus outward—for people in their community, and then to share their vision for their communities. Imagine how powerful your vision can become when a team of like-minded leaders is vision-casting for an entire community!

We urge the church leaders to understand that these aren't just their own "nice thoughts" for people. The visions the teams share are pieces of *God's vision* for their church and community!

This is the secret to vision. It isn't just our own dreams and ambitions for our church and community. True vision is God's vision for our churches, our neighborhoods, and our cities. He puts these things on our hearts when we train ourselves to listen. It's already there, but we must mine it out.

Ask yourself right now what you would say to your "Amandas." Start playing the Amanda Game with people you see in your church and people you pass in your everyday life—the single mom at the grocery store, the pierced barista at the coffee shop, the homeless man on the corner with his cardboard sign.

What is God's vision for these people? Mine it out of your spirit and then continue this practice every day. Play the game with your fellow church leaders and then compare notes. When you look at the commonalities, you'll begin to see a vision take shape.

Don't be discouraged or intimidated by setting a vision for your church. Vision isn't a scary word. It isn't ill-defined and vaporous, hard to grasp, and easy to lose. It isn't something to go find; it's something we discover in our spirits. It's in the heart of God. He offers it to your spirit through His Spirit, and He's waiting for you to draw it out and act on it.

As a side note, little seven-year-old Amanda has since graduated from high school as her class's valedictorian and is in medical school. At her speech to her graduating class, she shared many of the same things that my friend said to her that Sunday. The funny thing is that since she was only seven years old at the time, she can't remember what he actually said—she only remembers standing up on a chair.

Yet at her speech, she unconsciously repeated the fulfillment of nearly everything in the vision he cast over her that day. That vision by her worried, over-awed pastor has proven to be from the heart of God for her.

What lives will you speak vision into today?

## PEOPLE: OBSTACLES OR ASSETS?

There's no single right way to develop or lead a church. If God takes a person and knits his or her heart together with a congregation, and they work together on a common goal built on a shared vision and inspired by the Spirit, that church is going to thrive. It doesn't need to look like any other church in the area. If the leader God has raised up and the people are together, a church can have an amazing impact. This is the power of sharing the glimpses of God's heart that you and your ministry team receive from playing the Amanda Game.

But we must ask this question: If our impact is less than we dreamed it would be, does our vision need to be recharged? It may need fresh life. After all, if a vision is our current understanding of God's preferred future but our vision is old and outdated, it's no longer current, is it?

As we endeavor to execute a vision for ourselves or for a body of believers, we'll face many challenges, any of which can derail or delay the vision. For better or worse, though it takes a group to pursue a corporate vision, the people within that group can be some of the biggest obstacles to achieving the vision. They can also be the biggest catalysts for achieving God's vision.

Everyone who has tried to lead nearly anyone to do almost anything knows that people won't always share your vision for your church. And when they don't, it can be trouble.

## DEVELOPING A GOD-INSPIRED VISION

God's vision for the church is always about people. It isn't about buildings, programs, or initiatives.

I like to ask people what they would want their church to be if failure weren't a factor. Most of the time, church leaders respond with programs, but a program isn't a vision. Other times, people respond by giving me a slogan. A vision isn't a slogan.

A vision catches God's dream for your church, which means that writing a good one must include the church's universal mission and the five functions God gave the first-century church. As you learn more about each of these in the following chapters, keep this in mind: You'll be casting vision for each of the functions, and they aren't multiple choice. A full vision for your church will incorporate love for God and love for others, and it will be lived out in the five functions: *connect, grow, serve, go,* and *worship.*

Your vision statement is your chance to define your church, but be aware: You may get exactly what you ask for! For example, a church with compassionate leaders had a vision to care for hurting people. They became a magnet for the broken and the brokenhearted, and many people received love and practical care. However, the church didn't have a clear vision to help these people grow to maturity and serve others. Soon the pastors and other leaders felt overwhelmed with all the needs! The church was wonderfully successful in connecting with hurting people, but they struggled with the other functions of a thriving church.

## ARE YOU WILLING TO CHANGE YOUR REALITY?

As we seek to develop God-inspired vision, we must recognize a few things that can prevent us from seeing possibilities and opportunities. These "blinders" may include denial, complacency, past successes, past failures, personal agendas, and generalized assumptions or preconceptions. A church that has had financial problems but is finally secure may be hesitant to take financial risks. A pastor who's an outstanding teacher may rely on his ability to draw a crowd instead of building a great team of leaders and volunteers. A church that has just gone through a building campaign may be too exhausted to do anything but rest for a season. In these and many other instances, people can lose their vision to do what God has called them to do.

The Acts 2 process is partly about eliminating these blinders, which is why honesty in the assessment phase and being Spirit-led are important. Quite frankly, it's a large part of why we need a process in the first place and why we put such an emphasis at the beginning of the book on being willing to change.

We must exchange blinders for spiritual lenses because how we perceive things shapes our current reality. Learning to look at life and change in the light of God's Word will help us see what God has purposed for us. Learning to listen to Him through His Word, the witness of the Holy Spirit, and godly counsel will help us discern His vision.

It's important to note that a God-inspired vision doesn't ignore truth or reality. We must be willing to honestly assess circumstances in order to bridge the gap between the present reality and the future possibilities of our vision.

A vision is our current understanding of God's preferred future, and that future is all about *people*. It doesn't ignore reality; it *changes* reality for those who are touched by the vision. Those same people can be the single biggest obstacle to the vision, but they're also its greatest assets.

The questions for each of us are twofold: "Are we willing to love and pray for those who resist vision, asking God to turn them from our greatest hindrances into our greatest allies?" and "Will we cast a vision they can buy into and become a part of?"

If we will, we can enable people to become empowered disciples who carry out the church's mission and God's vision on the earth.

# 10 CORE VALUES

If the mission is universal and our vision is how each church can implement that mission, core values are like a church's personality. Core values are what set us apart—as an individual or as a church. For a body of believers, core values are like DNA: They're the unique combination of ingredients that give a church its identity. They also provide boundaries and parameters for how a church behaves.

A church's set of core values gives its members a sense of direction and awareness of what matters most to their church. The values drive priorities; shape behaviors, attitudes, and actions; direct processes; govern relationships; and articulate what the church stands for. More than mission or vision, core values tell those inside and outside the congregation what's distinctive and important about that church.

Churches focus their energies on their core values because these are most dear to their calling and vision. Similarly, values establish priorities for how churches go about ministering to people.

In *Ministry Nuts and Bolts*, Aubrey Malphurs expands this idea by observing, "Core values are fundamental to all that the organization does. They are ministry defining and have everything to do with a ministry's distinctiveness. They are what distinguishes one ministry from another, and they explain why some people are attracted to your church while others are repelled."[8]

Previously, we mentioned how the power of togetherness begins with just one individual. Interestingly, values help determine when a person will buy into a vision and get involved. Malphurs goes on to say that values "dictate personal involvement. If an individual's core values align with the ministry's core values, that individual is more likely to invest his or her life in that ministry."

Our core values are those things we believe are important and we demonstrate in our *behaviors*. When they truly buy in, a congregation will live out a church's core values in their daily lives. It isn't enough to state values; our true priorities are those things we both speak *and* live.

Every church has the ability to cast vision, but if the values can't support the vision or aren't being lived, that vision will fail. Eventually, the church will create another vision statement, but without strong values they won't fulfill this vision either because they haven't learned an important lesson: How we act determines where we go.

## DOERS OF THE WORD

While each church establishes its identity through its unique combination of core values, some values are nonnegotiable parts of the biblical Acts 2 model. We must never abandon our foundational doctrines. As some denominations and ministers in our nation are challenging bedrock principles, we must reaffirm our commitment to core biblical principles: We are committed to fulfill the Great Commission and the Great Commandment, and that's completely and thoroughly Pentecostal.

This includes but covers more than just style of worship—it's about the gifts of the Spirit disseminated at Pentecost, which are wonderful, necessary, and biblical. But so is Pentecostal fruit—love, joy, peace, forbearance, kindness, goodness, faithfulness, gentleness, and self-control. A church must be empowered and anointed if we expect individuals to be. We must never depend on programs, plans, and procedures alone but on the power of the Holy Spirit. As leaders, we can model incorporating the supernatural with the pragmatic.

If we're truly people of the Book, we must be doers of the Word as well as hearers. This doesn't just include the popular, socially acceptable gospel. It also means we tackle the difficult issues and the controversial standards—with love and grace but firmly and unequivocally.

While some who have walked away from their traditional values discount or cover up the sins of the flesh, we keep in mind that sins of the spirit can be just as destructive, if not more so. David's adultery with Bathsheba and the subsequent murder of her husband were horrendous sins, but the consequences of those sins pale in comparison to the consequences of his pride when he numbered the people to feed his own ego. Seventy thousand people died because of that pride, and we must be just as quick to embrace repentance and restorative healing for the oftentimes less obvious sins of the spirit as we are for the more blatant sins of the flesh.

We must not allow people who embrace an unrepentant lifestyle of pride, jealousy, and gossip to destroy our churches. Insidious, undermining issues like mean-spiritedness, divisiveness, and protracted and unrepentant anger have no place in our congregations or in our pulpits. Conversely, demonstrations of grace, mercy, and repentance show people that we understand

We may teach what we know, but we'll reproduce who we *are*.

human frailties and our focus is on restoration, not finger-pointing.

We carry a particular burden to model this as leaders because our own failings can be magnified in the pulpit. We may teach what we know, but we'll reproduce who we *are*.

## RELATIONSHIPS MAKE US BETTER

We've spent considerable time talking about the relational component of truth, and I believe it's essential that our churches embrace relational vitality. Relationship isn't only a key to reaching Millennials and future generations; it's also a vital component for building agreement within churches and between denominations. We may never totally agree on everything stylistically, but we can embrace the spirit of agreement. It's possible for us to disagree about nonessential components—without becoming disagreeable! All Christians are part of one big family.

We must desire to make one another better, to be resources for one another instead of impediments. Recent statistics show that an increasing number of pastors don't feel they have friends with whom they can talk freely and share their deepest concerns, fears, or temptations. This type of isolation sets them up for potential failure. What would happen if we embraced the core value of open, vital relationships that build bridges instead of erect walls?

## DISCOVERING YOUR CORE VALUES

In the Acts 2 Journey, we walk church leaders through the process of developing their core values. Remember, core values are your church's identity, so it's important to take the time to pick four or five beliefs or principles that your church strongly embraces.

Next, list the top six to eight greatest strengths of your church. What related behaviors make these things strengths? The idea is to find the values a church holds based on behavior. When you have a list of values, strengths, and behaviors, you have the basic components to discover your church's core values.

Church leaders will tell us what their core values are, such as being missions-oriented or Spirit-empowered, winning souls or pursuing transparency and accountability. They may tell us how much they give to missions or the emphasis they put on teaching new believers about the baptism of the Holy Spirit.

We then challenge them to give examples of behaviors in their churches that are *holding them back* from maximizing these strengths. It's one thing to determine what you think your church is about; it's another entirely to identify the changes necessary to go from where you are to where you want to be.

After leaders have identified the unhealthy behaviors, we ask them to talk about behaviors they would like to embrace in the future. When they've defined these behaviors, they have a clearer picture not only of where their church is but what is holding them back and where they would like to go in the future. The results of these three exercises form the genesis of a core-value statement.

## WRITE YOUR VALUES

It's a powerful technique to write out your values over the course of multiple retreats with a dream team of church leaders, and I encourage you to do this exercise—together with other leaders from your church if possible—as you read this book. Take a few moments to jot down some current strengths of your church, and then ask yourself what behaviors make these things strengths for the church you lead. Write down what behaviors are holding your church back, and then list some behaviors you would like to embrace moving forward.

As you write, the core values of your church will emerge. Like me, you may have subconsciously known what takes shape on the page. However, what I lacked was the process.

It isn't enough to be aware of core values subconsciously. If you want them to help your church stand for something, you must write them down and help others to grasp them.

What you write may look something like this: "We desire to be a learning church, a loving church, a praying church, a humble church, a supernatural church, a unified church, a generous church, a committed church, a fun church, a worshipping church, an influential church, and an outward-focused church."

Whatever your church's core values are, their unique shape and priority are what give your church its individual identity. When you become more aware of them and actively embrace them, you give your priesthood of believers a church identity they can truly embrace and own.

A church without core values can be influenced by the loudest voices and will try to be all things to all people, but this is a recipe for being too spread out and scattered to be truly effective. Your church will continually be presented with opportunities. People will present you with causes and ways to spend your money and your time. If you haven't identified your core values, these people will get you offtrack with all manner of things.

Your core values will dictate how you spend your time, ministry resources, and money. With clearly defined values you'll know clearly what is most important to your church.

The fact is that nearly every church has core values. However, many haven't written them down, although this simple process is extremely valuable.

Remember that your vision for your church will

> Your church will only be as strong as the values that support it.

only be as strong as the values that support it. A train can only go as fast as the tracks will permit it, and a river is only as powerful as the banks that contain it. When a train goes too fast for its tracks, it derails; when a river overflows its banks, the surrounding land floods. The behaviors your church practices must be able to support the vision you cast or the results will end in disaster.

We see the same principle in a leader's character—if the flaws in a person's character undermine their ministry, it shows that they aren't maturing spiritually. The values revealed by your church's behaviors illustrate your potential.

Don't underestimate how important this is. Grasping your core values doesn't block you in or put limits on you. Values show you the path forward to fulfill your vision; but if you don't create clear core values this will sabotage the rest of your process.

## CONFUSION LEADS TO CONFLICT

We have seen many leaders become confused about their core values. It isn't unusual for a church to confuse core values with ministry models, programs, traditions, and practices.

For instance, a church may say, "We value small groups," but they may not recognize that groups are a ministry model, not a core value. While ministry models can provide a cohesive approach to ministry, putting too much emphasis on the model can lock the congregation into a model even as the real value ebbs away.

It's important to reassess periodically what made a ministry model valuable. We must ask what made it part of the church's DNA in the first place and question honestly whether or not that's still the case. When you answer these questions, you can rediscover the core values *behind* ministry models.

Successful programs often end up on a church's list of core values, as well. However, programs exist for a purpose, and if we examine that purpose, the core value is often underneath. The church may say, "We value Royal Rangers," when the real reason they chose to implement the program was to minister to the next generation of young men in the congregation. We must be careful that our values focus on *why* we do what we do, not on the method or program itself.

While most churches wouldn't list a tradition as a core value, a church's behavior can clearly demonstrate this perspective. A church might say they never deviate from their service order, thinking consistency demonstrates a cherished value. But when we continue patterns without purpose, those traditions have overtaken our values. Such a condition won't let a church respond effectively to changing needs. Questioning traditions and whether they have outlived their purpose and are limiting the church's ability to meet changing needs helps us remove them from the altar and replace them with more responsive value systems.

Church practices communicate what we value but aren't intrinsically core values. Healthy churches are intentional about living true values and making ministry adjustments to fit those values rather than making their values fit their practices.

## CORE VALUES VS. PERSONAL PREFERENCE

A friend of mine pastored a church that had signs in the front of the parking lot reserving certain parking spots for senior adults. Additional signs in the auditorium signaled that the front row of chairs was reserved for seniors.

My friend was a relatively new pastor at this church, and one night at a meeting of deacons, one of the older church leaders passionately shared his heart to reach young people. He was a high school teacher, and God moved his heart as he saw students every day in the hallway. "Pastor, we've got to find a way to reach kids," he said with deep conviction.

Toward the end of the meeting, my pastor friend asked if there was anything else for the group to discuss. The man who was so passionate about teenagers spoke up and said that there was a problem.

"Some of our teenagers are sitting in the front seats that are reserved for senior adults, and we need to do something about that," the man said.

No one said anything for a time, but while my friend didn't want to offend this elder, he felt he needed to point out the obvious. The pastor said, "You know, in every church where I've been in the past, we thought it was a good thing that the teenagers sat in the front row."

The man actually got up and walked out of the room. The rest of the people in the meeting sat around looking at one another for a few moments before wrapping up the final few pieces of business.

About five minutes later, the man came back in—carrying all the plastic signs from the chairs. He tossed them in the trashcan and looked at the pastor. "You don't know where those went," he said with a smile.

Sometimes, what we're passionate about isn't what people see. That church was undergoing a transition: They were passionate about reaching young people, but their signals sent a message to young visitors that the focus was on seniors, not youth. The church kept its parking lot signs because it was interested in honoring older believers, but their tradition needed to catch up with their core values.

Sometimes, what seems like a core value may actually be something completely different—a personal preference or "conviction." While people in our churches don't typically think in terms of core values, they definitely understand *convictions*. True biblical convictions are boundaries for our core values that are created by Scripture and directed by the Holy Spirit.

However, it's possible for core values to be disconnected or wrongly derived from Scripture, and in these cases, unhealthy convictions can take over. These convictions aren't as connected to the Holy Spirit as we may suppose, and they often stem from personal issues and wounds masked as personal convictions. When leaders fail to discern the differences between biblical convictions and personal convictions, dominant voices (or silent influencers) can redirect a church's vision and move it in unhealthy directions.

Biblical absolutes, community standards, and personal convictions are all subject to scriptural directives and should supplant

> When churches don't operate with strong, established core values, people within the church can easily substitute their personal preferences and convictions.

personal beliefs and behaviors. However, when churches don't operate with strong, established core values, people within the church can easily substitute their personal preferences and convictions. These beliefs are deeply ingrained and develop over a person's lifetime and Christian journey. They are rarely questioned, are unwritten, and are typically invisible until conflict arises with the church's vision.

When personal preferences and convictions replace core values, a leader's efforts often shift to focus on making people happy—and to giving in to what is unhealthy by allowing immature Christians to dictate the leadership direction of the church. Some examples of this may include a worship style, seasonal or calendar events, the role and authority of the pastor, leadership or control by certain individuals or families, and other minor theological positions.

## I JUST CAME TO HAVE CHURCH

I told you in the beginning of this book that when I first went to First Assembly in North Little Rock, I had never done much "pastoring"—lots of preaching, but none of the pastoral duties that are so common. I had also never led a body of believers in more than a song.

When I arrived at First Assembly, they wanted to know if I was going to push for a building program. My answer was, "I didn't come to build a building. I came to have church."

The previous pastor had been there only a year before leaving. His predecessor had been there three years, and his predecessor had been there five years. This trend was alarming, and I was thirty-nine with no experience. I wasn't eager to dive into a building program with a plateaued church and uncertain footing, and I felt like I was under a lot of pressure to make people happy. Different parties in the church tried to exert their influence, and I knew I had to resist the temptation to let their personal preferences set the church's direction.

The pastor who had been there three years had talked the church into buying property—it passed by one vote—but the dissension from that never calmed down, and he didn't survive. The next pastor didn't like the property and wanted new property, but some of the congregants, who had not liked the property previously, now liked it and *disliked* him for wanting something new. Out he went as well.

I had walked into a mess!

However, the church soon began to grow. We moved to two services. The bottom line is that they talked me into moving forward with a new building.

Needless to say, some of the older congregants didn't like the idea of change—especially the eldest living charter member whom we affectionately called Mamma Gregg. She didn't attend church too often because she was frail, but she only lived a half block away in her little white frame house. Several of her friends lived close by in two high rise apartments designed for seniors.

I knew she was resistant so I thought I would walk over and convince her. As I came in, she said, "Pastor, are you going to stay with us at our church, or are you going to go with them to that new church?"

"Mamma Gregg," I said, "you know, there's only going to be one church. We're all going to go."

"Oh, no," she said, "you don't understand." She looked at me firmly and said, "The glory resides at 22$^{nd}$ and Franklin." (This was the location of the existing building.)

I tried to explain to her that this wasn't my vision—that the church had owned the property long before I got there—and that it was the church's vision to move. She said, "You all may go, but some of us aren't leaving. We're staying right here."

I tried again: "Mamma Gregg, everybody is going to the new building."

She said, "Well, I just want to know, are you going to pastor them, or are you going to pastor us?"

We went back and forth like this for a time, and then she finally fixed me with her pale eyes and said, "You may go, and there may be a lot of people who go with you, but let me promise you one thing. When you get over there to that new building, 'Icky-bod' (this was how she pronounced Ichabod) is going to be writ on the door."

How could I argue with the oldest living charter member? I left, frustrated and uncertain how I could win her over—and how much influence she would have.

As I walked out with my youth pastor, Charlie, he asked, "Why didn't you explain it to her?"

"Why don't *you* go back in there and explain it to her?" I countered.

He wisely declined.

How was I going to lead this woman—and her sixty or so friends who felt the same way—to support the move to our new location? I didn't want to argue with her, so I prayed instead.

Eventually, God gave me an idea. We had bought a big people mover—a van to help transport people the five miles to the new building—and we picked up a group of the older people from the retirement communities near the church and bought them dinner at a cafeteria. After the dinner, we took them over to the new site where all we had was a concrete slab. On that slab was a chalk outline.

It showed them where the classroom was for their Sunday school class. I talked to them about the church and the vision and I said, "Now, I can't point to you where my office is going to be. I don't even know exactly where the nursery is going to be or where the youth room is going to be. But I know where your classroom is going to be. It's right here."

I worked to ease their fears and show them we wouldn't leave them behind.

Construction on the new building was completed and the time to move arrived.

At the final service in the old building, Mamma Gregg made it to church. People had been getting up and saying how excited they were about the new location, and then Mamma Gregg appeared, wheeled to the front by her son, Paul.

She wanted to say something.

I was mortified. I was certain she was going to suck the joy out of the room by pronouncing that "Icky-bod" would be writ on the door. But I couldn't deny the eldest living charter member!

I walked over and handed her the mike. "Number one," she said, just dragging it out, "always pay your tithe." I wondered where that came from and clapped and cheered. But she had more to say. *Dear Lord, here it comes, I thought.* I could almost hear the drum roll before the firing squad.

Pausing for dramatic effect, she finally said, "Always follow our pastor wherever God leads him."

She sealed the deal right there. The elderly people within her sphere of influence could have caused division within the church—and no doubt would have. It could have derailed the entire vision for the church.

Instead, God turned that moment into a chance to unify our body behind a single vision going forward, and it was partly because one woman bought into it.

No matter how much you think people have disagreed with you and no matter how much you think they're trying to destroy the vision, sometimes it isn't the vision but the price and the pace that frighten people or cause division.

Often, people are just *afraid*. They may want to buy into the vision but they're afraid it's going to cost them too much or is happening too fast. Mamma Gregg and other older saints were resistant to change because they didn't know where it would leave them—and whether it would leave them *out*.

You can't argue and rationalize with fear. With Mamma Gregg, I had to bring her friends around her to help her understand and accept the vision. I had to assure them that the pace and the price were going to be okay, and that they weren't going to be left behind.

Mostly, though, I had to pray—because nothing short of the Holy Spirit was going to change that sister's mind at her age!

The temptation to let their personal preferences set the direction of the church was strong in those early years, but I had to remain firm and cling to the vision God had given me for the church.

You'll face people who want to influence the direction of the church, your decisions, and the church's values. It's important to have a trusted team, co-ministers of the gospel, working beside you, but be wary of letting anyone overly influence you or the church.

Pastors have a responsibility to set down clear values for the rest of the church, and when combined with our universal mission and God's vision for our churches, we can create church environments that foster ownership, discipleship, and growth.

Hopefully you took this opportunity to write down your church's core values, because in the next chapter we'll put your mission, vision, and core values together into a strategic plan to get your church from where it is to where you want it to be.

# UNIT III
# BECOMING AN
# ACTS 2 CHURCH

# 11 BALANCING THE SPIRITUAL AND THE STRATEGIC

The question you must answer is: "Does God have a plan for my church—or not?" If you agree with me that God has a plan for every church, the next question is equally important: "Is the Holy Spirit willing to share it with me?"

The entire Acts 2 process is built on the understanding that God has a plan and the Holy Spirit wants to reveal it to us. Why *wouldn't* He want to share with you the direction He has for your church?

This all fits in with what we've done in the last few chapters—construct a framework to receive from God. The process isn't God's plan, but it *is* the avenue and the method for mining His plan.

We established that our mission is universal, we began to build a vision around people, and we identified the core values and behaviors that reflect those values. Now, it's time to put it all together into a strategic plan that will help you get from where you are (your values) to where you want to go (your vision).

Now we return to the five biblical functions of the first-century church. Described in detail in Acts 2:42–47, these functions form the pathway from values to vision. The five functions are actually a template you can use to develop a plan for your church, so consider this chapter a primer, introducing you to these functions as a way to help you discover God's plan.

However, before we get into the functions, we must recognize that without Holy Spirit empowerment in our churches, the mission, vision, values, and plans merely amount to programs. Before we talk further about a strategy for building a plan from the five functions, it's important to understand that any strategic plan finds its genesis in the inspiration of the Holy Spirit. We must focus first on becoming inspired (think about the indwelled disciples and Peter's preaching on Pentecost) and reinvigorated—only then will we have the necessary power and perspective to implement any sort of strategy.

The odd thing is that in some churches, we see resistance to calls for revitalization while others resist the idea of planning. Some don't see the need for the work of the Holy Spirit or feel their churches have enough of the Spirit already, and others act like the Holy Spirit has no place in a planning meeting. The truth is that we need Him in every component of our lives and churches.

Every church can use more of the Spirit. Needing revitalization doesn't necessarily imply your church is dead and lifeless. Whatever the condition of our church, we can all cry with Isaiah, "Oh, that You would rend the heavens! That You would come down! That the mountains might shake at Your presence . . . to make Your name known to Your adversaries, that the nations may tremble at Your presence! When You did awesome things for which we did not look, You came down, the mountains shook at Your presence" (Isa. 64:1–3).

In speaking to John the Baptist's followers, Jesus explained how He was revitalizing the Jews: The blind saw, the lame walked, the lepers were cleansed, and the deaf heard. The dead rose up, and people received the gospel. Then He said something curious: "And blessed is he who is not offended because of Me" (Matt. 11:6).

That is the message we would give to each and every church: Blessed is the church that is not offended because of Him.

We do ourselves a great disservice if we think that because we're in a Spirit-filled church we have nothing to gain by praying for, seeking, and expecting revitalization. We can miss out if we assume we're already as full of the Holy Spirit in our personal lives and services as we can be. Don't be offended by this talk of revitalization if you're in a church that's already experiencing the Holy Spirit. Instead, see this as an opportunity to bring it to a higher spiritual level by being hungry for more of Him!

In addition, don't think that the Holy Spirit has no place in a strategic plan because the Spirit who can inspire us spontaneously is the same Spirit who helps us learn God's plans for our churches.

## SPIRIT AND STRATEGY IN HARMONY

One of the churches that participated in the Acts 2 Journey had an amazing and unique story—a case study in what can happen when the Spirit and the strategic work together.

When we began working with them, there were exactly twenty-eight people in the congregation. Interestingly, fifteen of them were high school students. The pastor had been a youth pastor, and this was his first lead role. The church was in a virtual ghost town, and the church building may have been the only functioning public building that remained in this particular community. The pastor had brought a team of people with him, and five of them were high school students. What further stood out about these students was that they were very intense in their prayers.

One of our Acts 2 team members visited their church on a Sunday morning for the prayer service that preceded the 10:15 a.m.

service. He arrived a little late because he missed a turn, but he walked into one of the most intense prayer meetings he had ever been in—and teenagers led it! The young man leading was a high school senior, and the atmosphere was like a youth camp, even though there were some older folks present as well. Students sat in the front rows of the church, and the older saints sat behind them supportively.

The dream team that came to the Acts 2 Journey consisted of the pastor, his wife, the dad of one of the students, and five high school students. Their dream team proceeded to build a plan together, and they were just as intense about building that plan as they were about praying before their services. They launched their plan right before several of the young people graduated from high school.

The students who graduated were leaving for college just as the fruit of their plan began to grow. Soon the church began to grow in health and numbers. All of the new people were unchurched families from the area, and the pastor found himself in need of basic discipleship tools because he had many people who had never opened a Bible before.

These were *exactly* the kind of people the students had dreamed of reaching!

Completely against prevailing trends, where young people leave their rural communities and never return, several of these students decided to change their college plans and go to school closer to home. They wanted to be a part of what God was doing in that church as a result of the plans they had helped to form.

This is a wonderful example of what can happen when the Spirit and the strategic come together in harmony. Having a plan doesn't replace passion for God; it shapes that passion into a focused plan and then executes it.

We sometimes act like anything from the Holy Spirit has to be last minute and that making plans is antithetical to being led by the Spirit. We confuse being Spirit-led with being spontaneous.

> Having a plan doesn't replace passion for God; it shapes that passion into a focused plan and then executes it.

Some leaders fail to realize that the same Holy Spirit who directs us in the moment can also inspire us during the planning stages. Worship services are terrific examples of this. Most worship leaders will plan out the songs they're going to sing even though they want their worship to be Spirit-led. The compromise is having a plan but remaining flexible; if the Spirit spontaneously puts a song on the worship leader's or pastor's heart, we must be able to flow with the change.

A vision without a plan to carry it out is nothing more than a dream. However, when we create our plans under the inspiration of the Holy Spirit, we position ourselves to catch God's plan for us and our churches.

## PEOPLE WITH A PLAN

The church in Acts 2 was a Spirit-filled church led by disciples who were Spirit-baptized and Spirit-directed. We read about their empowerment in Acts 2:4: "And they were all filled with the Holy Spirit and began to speak with other tongues, as the Spirit gave them utterance." Peter later confirmed that this was what the prophet Joel had described—God was pouring out His Spirit on all flesh (see Acts 2:14–21). This outpouring was what the disciples had waited for; it was the promised power to witness (Acts 1:8).

This was God's plan for His people on earth. Contrary to some thinking, the presence and flow of the Holy Spirit doesn't imply a complete loss of order. God established a *plan* for His Spirit-empowered church, and we can read about it in Acts 2:42–47, which clarifies the functions or activities of the newly formed church. The plan hinged on fellowship, discipleship, gift-oriented ministry, evangelism, and worship. (It's interesting to note that revival is what the church first experiences; evangelism is what the church then engages in. Revival is periodic; evangelism is continuous. Revival cannot last; evangelism must not stop.)

God does nothing out of order. There's a divine purpose in all He does. Similarly, He didn't establish a pattern on this earth devoid of order and motivated only by how we individually interpret the Spirit's promptings. No, God had something in mind, and because we have His blueprint, we are people of that plan.

When you've established your mission, vision, and values, it's time to develop a strategic plan based on God's model. If your vision is where you or your church are going in the next three to five years and your core values determine your actions and your identity, then the strategic plan is how you get from where you are (values) to where you want to go (vision). We build a strategic plan around the functions of the church: *connect, grow, serve, go,* and *worship.*

A congregation is like people in a car. Our vision of the preferred future is where we are going. Our mission is why we're going on the journey together. *Connect, grow, serve, go,* and *worship* are what is going on inside the car, and our values and chosen priorities are the rules of the road and the road itself. Finally, the strategic plan is *how* we're going to get to our preferred future.

We go forward with both the power of the Spirit and a plan.

## COMMUNITY PASTORS

One of the more interesting Act 2 Journey stories resulted from a scholarship to the Journey that I gave away at a gathering in Phoenix. I said that the first one who got up to the

> We go forward with both the power of the Spirit and a plan.

front would get the scholarship, and a guy in the front row ran forward immediately. His wife, Kassie, was actually the pastor, but she and Greg were both Bible school graduates who were pastoring in a little town in the mountains of northeastern Arizona—a place where people go to hide from the government.

The community consisted predominantly of heavily armed survivalists or extreme Mormons, and, for a host of reasons, 60 of the 180 children in the elementary school had no official address. Many people didn't have Social Security numbers because they were living off the grid.

It's difficult to establish a church there because the people are afraid to be known. Imagine trying to build a church in a place where as soon as you get to know people a little bit, they disappear into hiding!

When Greg and Kassie received the scholarship, the church had seven people in it—not even large enough to engage in the Journey. But we determined that their scholarship would include paying for one of our team members to go out there for a weekend to help them build a strategy. He went out for the weekend, met with the couple, and discovered that they were a great, praying, and passionate couple. Still, it was difficult to come up with a plan for how they could effectively minister to their community.

One of the seven people in the church was a woman who taught fifth grade at the elementary school where they met for Sunday services. They began to build a plan around the idea of connecting to the community through its children. In fact, the goal was *not* to build the church at all. The plan that came together was for this couple to become pastors of the community. They realized they might never get people to come to their church, so they would go to the people.

The strategy centered on partnering with the elementary school, and the pastor and her husband sought to respond to members of the community in moments when they needed spiritual help.

The following year, this little church was incredibly excited to have more than thirty people in attendance on Easter Sunday. The best part was that nearly two dozen people come forward for salvation! A couple of years later, Greg went to work for a drug and alcohol rehabilitation program as a counselor and chaplain. Kassie pastors the church and works in a convenience store, but throughout that community they are known as Pastor Kassie and Pastor Greg. Everyone knows where to turn when they need spiritual help.

Having a plan was a key element in this amazing story. Although our traditional thinking dictated that the church was too small for the Acts 2 Journey, it wasn't too small for God! He had to reveal a plan to us because "traditional thinking" wasn't going to work in that community. Their plan required a revival in their thinking, and the Holy Spirit led them to an unconventional solution for reaching lives.

## THE PLAN IS ABOUT PEOPLE

The strategic plan's primary focus should be to nurture people to become that God wants them to be—not merely to facilitate our programs. The strategic plan uses the programs and ministries of the church, but remember this point: It's all about the people.

A vision takes the mission and biblical systems of the church and articulates them towards a preferred future, communicating where the church is going. In the next few chapters, we'll spend more time on these biblical functions as part of the process that takes us from where we are to where we want to be. Your challenge will be to define what each of the five functions means for your church in order to develop a vision statement for each.

Using the template of the five biblical functions, you'll begin to uncover God's plan. For many pastors and leaders, this will be the clearest plan that you've ever completed for your church, and that's what makes this so unique and amazing. The model from Acts 2 isn't about constricting churches; it's about helping them hear from God and providing a template to articulate His plan.

# 12 CONNECT

In our current context, *connect* is about far more than fellowship. It's also about hospitality and welcoming visitors warmly so they want to return and become a part of your body of believers. It's about our horizontal relationships with other people, but it's also about our vertical relationship with God. The better an individual's and a church's relationship with God, the better their relationships will be with others.

Love among believers isn't optional; it's essential and central to God's calling for the church. On the night Jesus was betrayed, one of His final instructions to His followers was about the nature of their relationships: "A new commandment I give to you, that you love one another; as I have loved you, that you also love one another. By this all will know that you are My disciples, if you have love for one another" (John 13:34–35).

John was paying attention that night. In his first letter, he captured the heart of Jesus' teaching: Our love for others flows naturally (or supernaturally) from our experience of Jesus' great love for us. "In this the love of God was manifested toward us, that God has sent His only begotten Son into the world, that we might live through Him. In this is love, not that we loved God, but that

He loved us and sent His Son to be the propitiation for our sins. Beloved, if God so loved us, we also ought to love one another" (1 John 4:9–11).

In building an Acts 2 church, love is the glue that holds everything together. In his book, *Natural Church Development*, Christian Schwarz comments, "Growing churches possess a measurably higher 'love quotient' than stagnant, declining ones. Healthy growing churches practice hospitality as believers invite others into their homes as a normal part of their Christian lives. People don't want to hear us talk about love, they want to experience how Christian love really works."[9]

The way you welcome and treat people who come into your church is the first piece of *connect*. This is that vital first impression, and, cliché or not, people establish a great deal of their opinion about your church the moment they walk through the doors—if they haven't already formed it in the parking lot! We simply can't overstate how important it is to welcome people warmly.

The second aspect of *connect* is helping the congregation live out an Acts 2-modeled lifestyle. At the beginning of the book, we read that the believers of the first-century church shared their lives with one another and supported, prayed for, and served one another.

Too often, our idea of fellowship is to talk with people before church or to get together for meals, but relationship is all-encompassing. Relationship in a biblical, Acts 2-framework is *sharing life*.

We can break down each of the five functions into components, but they aren't linear and separate. They intersect with one another, and they share this in common: They must be lived out in relationship. We start with connect—not because it's the most important but because discipleship, service, evangelism, and worship happen in the context of relationship.

## WHERE DOES CONNECT BEGIN?

It's widely reported that over 100 million people attend church every Sunday, but more rigorous research shows the number is only about 50 million.[10] However, most of those people have never answered one very important question: *Why?*

Some go out of guilt. Some go because they feel pressured by family members. Some attend church merely out of habit. Some go because they think it's "the thing to do."

Tragically, millions more avoid church attendance for a variety of reasons: They think the sermons are boring, the people aren't friendly, all the preacher wants is their money, they need Sunday to rest and spend time with family, and so forth. Many never darken a church door because they think they don't need God and they don't want anything to do with religion.

Yet many people have never clarified to themselves *why* they make this choice.

If an individual who doesn't attend church were to ask members of your congregation why they go to church, would your members be ready with an answer? What would they say?

Before we welcome people to church and before we help them get plugged in to grow and serve, we must first invite them. And how will we invite them if we ourselves don't know why we go? Reaching out to the unchurched begins with one simple thing: connecting to others and welcoming them to our family.

## ALL IN THE FAMILY

The moment you were born, you became part of the human race and a family. When you were reborn spiritually, you were born into *God's* family. Peter writes, "God has given us the privilege of being born again so that we are now members of God's own family" (1 Peter 1:3).

What is the name of this family? The Bible says this family is called the church.

The church isn't an institution. It isn't a business. It isn't a social club. *Connect* recognizes the church as a *family*—a family Paul calls the "the support and foundation of the truth" (1 Tim. 3:15). As church leaders it's our job to help facilitate this, which helps the members of our congregations form relationships with one another.

Jesus told us that in this life, we will have trouble. The storms of life will come—personal storms, financial storms, relational storms, physical, and health storms. If you don't have a good foundation and some support, those storms are going to wash away whatever you've built in your life. The church exists on the earth to share the gospel and to be a support and foundation upon which we can build our lives and relationships by facilitating people's relationship with the Rock, Jesus Christ.

> The Christian life is more than belief and action—it's relationship.

The Christian life is more than belief and action—it's relationship. It's connection, belonging, and community.

Family.

Sometimes I hear people say, "I'm a Christian, but I don't need a church." That's like saying you want to play football in the NFL but you don't want to be part of a team, or you want to be a soldier but not be in an army, or you want to play a tuba but not be in an orchestra.

A Christian without a church family is an orphan. Orphans lack the support and foundation necessary to make it through

rough times, and they grow up disassociating with society, feeling burdened by trust issues, and missing out on the power and support of family.

It's a tragic thing to be orphaned—to be left without family. It's worse to actively choose to be an orphan, yet millions do so every Sunday while we sit in our pews, oblivious to the plight of "orphans" around the world.

## A MEANS OF CHANGING LIVES

In his book, *Connecting*, professional therapist Larry Crabb brings a unique and insightful perspective on the potential power of the church.

> I have strong reason to suspect that Christians sitting dutifully in church congregations, for whom 'going to church' means doing a variety of spiritual activities, have been given resources that, if released, could powerfully heal broken hearts, overcome the damage done by abusive backgrounds, encourage the depressed to courageously move forward, stimulate the lonely to reach out, revitalize discouraged teens and children with new and holy energy, and introduce hope into the lives of the countless people who feel rejected, alone, and useless.[11]

That's a powerful vision for the family of God. Crabb describes a hoped-for day in which "God's people, ordinary Christians whose lives regularly intersect, will accomplish most of the good that we now depend on mental health professionals to provide. And they will do it by connecting with each other in ways that only the gospel makes possible."

Paul told Timothy that the church is "joined and held together by every supporting ligament." Paul went on to say the church is designed so it "grows and builds itself up in love, as each part does its work" (Ephesians 4:16 NIV). I believe we haven't fully developed the "work" Paul describes of supporting and connecting with one another.

What if we changed the way we look at church, do church, and provide in church? Instead of focusing on what we can get out of it, what if we participated in this family as a means of changing lives?

Imagine what that would mean to a person's life when everything is falling apart. Could it mean that we could help them hold it together by supporting them? I believe this is the nature of the "work" Paul was talking about—that of supporting joints and ligaments that help hold one another up when injured and hurting.

What if we saw church as a way of bringing people who are far away from Him closer to Jesus, in whose presence we are healed, accepted, loved, and nurtured—often through human hands, feet, and smiles?

Crabb observes, "I see a healing community as a group of people who place connecting at the exact center of their purpose and passion—connecting with God (worship), connecting with others (loving service), and connecting with ourselves (personal wholeness)."[12]

When a church is focused on loving God and loving others, *connect, grow, serve, go,* and *worship* take on a whole new light.

This dream isn't Crabb's alone—it's always been part of God's plan.

## CONNECTING IS GOD'S DESIGN

Have you ever stopped to ask why God designed the church? Take a moment to honestly consider it. Two answers are readily apparent to me: for His glory and for humankind's benefit. One of the most powerful ways we connect with Him and with one another is in the context of a church family.

The church fulfills many purposes, and it can be constructive to examine every ministry, vision, core value, and strategy to ensure they are fulfilling these purposes. Let's look at how church helps us feel God, face our problems, fill up, give back, and fulfill our mission in life.

One of the most foundational purposes of church is helping us experience God. We can easily go all day without even thinking about Him—even people who've been Christians many years! God knows we have a tendency to lose focus on Him, so He created a Sabbath for us to pause, rest, and refocus on Him. The Bible promises blessings for keeping the Sabbath (see Isa. 58:13).

Experiencing God refocuses us. We have a word for this experience—*worship*.

A sad truth is that many people have never felt God because they've never truly worshipped Him. Worship is honoring God with extravagant love and extreme submission, creating an environment in which we intimately connect with God vertically. This can be amazing when we do so with other believers with whom we are connected horizontally.

> Experiencing God refocuses us. We have a word for this experience—*worship*.

Worship's purpose is to glorify and honor God. When we refocus like this, it changes our perspective on our problems and lives because it helps us focus on how great He is.

While music is only one component of worship (we'll discuss this further in a later chapter), it's perhaps the most important.

Music provides a vehicle that helps us focus our attention on God and on the act of worship, orienting our hearts toward Him. Music stirs our souls in amazing ways; it truly is a gift from the Lord. When we use the creative power of music to worship our Creator, we can experience Him in a way that ties us in with the rest of creation. He is constantly worshipped around His heavenly throne, and it's a privilege to join our songs to the melodies of heaven.

## FIND HELP IN TIMES OF TROUBLE

Earlier, we established that church is to be a pillar and a foundation. Without it, our lives are exposed when the storms come. Someone has rightly said that you're either in a problem right now, have just come out of one, or are ready to go into one. This may sound pessimistic, but it's actually realistic—the optimism is in how we handle the problems, not in whether or not we have them. We can all get discouraged, fatigued, and drained, and in these times, more so than in others, we must be able to turn to something sturdy and reliable.

While we can turn to God in prayer individually, He knows it's important for us to have resources with flesh on (others). He wants those people to be from our church family. According to Paul, we are to encourage each other and give each other strength (see 1 Thess. 5:10–11). Larry Crabb puts this in his unique perspective:

> When two people connect . . . something is poured out of one and into the other that has the power to heal the soul of its deepest wounds and restore it to health. People experience the life-changing force of healing relationships when something powerful comes out of one and touches something good in another.[13]

We don't want to face problems alone but often we don't know how to ask for help. At these times, even more so than others, we need a church family. From the loss of a loved one, to a negative report from the doctor, to marriage problems, we need strong support during the storms of life.

A church isn't supposed to be a social club or a common meeting place; it's supposed to be family—a loving, living community. Yes, we come together to worship God, but we also come together to connect with one another. Where better to find encouraging and godly friends than within a church family? Would we rather find our friends at work, among the neighbors, or in some other setting? There are certainly wonderful people in those settings, but the people we worship and fellowship with are uniquely qualified to bear us up during times of trouble and to encourage our relationship with God.

We need one another—we can't make it through life alone. The Devil likes nothing better than to isolate us, cutting us out from the herd when we are weakest and most vulnerable. Like any predator, he seeks to inflict his damage when we're isolated.

Peter put it like this: "You should be like one big happy family, full of sympathy toward each other, loving one another with tender hearts" (1 Peter 3:8 TLB). Simply being friendly isn't enough to bind us together; we must make deep, meaningful friendships because compassion flows out of friendship.

## AN ENVIRONMENT FOR GROWTH AND DISCIPLESHIP

The purpose of church isn't to help people have a good time but to help them mature and grow in their faith, being discipled and discipling others in turn.

The church disciples people by encouraging belief, teaching knowledge, and facilitating relationship—all in love. When you belong to a church family where the Word is emphasized, it will build up your faith, clarify your values, and develop your character.

However, the Christian life is more than just theory. It can't simply be taught from a pulpit; it must be lived out. There are only a few places where this can happen, and church is one of the best because we can do so among other members of our church family who are growing and maturing as well. Where better to practice forgiving those who have hurt you, to learn to make difficult decisions with wisdom and the leading of the Holy Spirit, to develop character necessary to be a good spouse, or to overcome a self-destructive behavior?

> God doesn't want us to remain spiritual infants; He wants us to mature. Our church family helps with that growth.

Practicing the teachings in God's Word within the context of a church family helps with those issues and many more. God doesn't want us to remain spiritual infants; He wants us to mature. Our church family helps with that growth.

While some people feel that attending the main service is sufficient, smaller groups are ideal for encouraging connection because so much growth can happen within these smaller contexts. Sunday school is an excellent place to bond with other believers and establish relationships, as is being in a small group that meets in homes and shares meals.

Church and its connected programs should help create environments for growth and discipleship. Whatever the setting, the objective is to have a systematic study of the Bible and have relationship with others for peer learning, encouragement, and accountability.

## GIVE BACK

Church is more than occupying a pew. God didn't plan for us to be consumers in the body of Christ without giving back. Think again of the priesthood of all believers' paradigm shift I mentioned earlier. God expects each believer to contribute to the body of Christ, and He has given us abilities, talents, gifts, and unique backgrounds that can help other people. Any time you use your talents or abilities to help someone you are ministering to that person.

Only a small percentage of Christians are called into the full-time ministry, but we're *all* called to minister. A Christian who isn't ministering is actually a contradiction. One day we'll stand before Christ and give an account of how we used the talents and gifts He gave us. That's why one of the major jobs of the church is to help people discover and develop their ministry and to provide a venue to help them give to others (we'll cover this in more depth in chapter 14).

Paul explained it like this: "For we are His workmanship, created in Christ Jesus for good works, which God prepared beforehand that we should walk in them" (Eph. 2:10). You aren't a mistake; you're a masterpiece, a work of art, truly one-of-a-kind. Even if your parents didn't plan your birth, God did. He designed you, and regardless of the circumstances of your birth, He wants you on this earth for a purpose. Your unique offering to the world is your *ministry*—the "good works" Paul mentioned.

God says to each and every one of us, "I want your life to count."

Various types of service or ministry combined with people who have various gifts operating in their lives form the body of

Christ. Each one of us is necessary (which can be countercultural in a world that teaches us we are nothing more than an upstart ape).

We can spend a great deal of money on therapy, self-help books, and motivational seminars, but all of these say the same things. They all want to improve your self-esteem, but the true key to healthy self-esteem is figuring out what God made you to be—and then being it. We do this best in community.

## COMPLETE THE MISSION

Related to but different from helping people find their ministries is the role of church in helping people fulfill their life's mission. If finding our ministry is learning what God made us to be and then being it, our life mission is the grand purpose for our lives.

In Acts 20:24, Paul spoke to the Ephesian elders for the last time, and he wanted them to grasp his driving purpose in life. He told them, "But nothing, not even my life, is more important than my completing my *mission*. This is nothing other than the ministry I received from the Lord Jesus: to testify about the good news of God's grace" (emphasis added, CEB).

Part of every Christian's life mission is the Great Commission. Someone once told us the good news, and now we are to pass it on. The Bible says we are ambassadors for Christ. Have you cared enough lately to tell someone the good news that Christ wants to forgive them of their sins? We must train our congregations to share this message so others can have a home in heaven and experience God's presence in this life.

Our life mission is to be *contagious*, infected with the life of Christ and spreading to a dying world. We accomplish this outward focus best together as a body with each part supplying its intended function.

## A PLACE TO MEET NEEDS

> Our life mission is to be contagious, infected with the life of Christ and spreading to a dying world.

God designed the church to help meet some of our most basic needs. We each want significance, need fellowship, desire stability, want a purpose, and crave inspiration.

If we don't look to meet these needs within a church family, we'll look to other sources. Where will we meet our need for significance, support, stability, self-expression, and stimulation? Our jobs may offer a form of significance, and being part of a neighborhood or community can offer support, but are these the most qualified, desirable people to meet our needs?

A church family is the best place to meet needs in a godly way. But here is the catch: The church flips our normal expectation on its head. Instead of being a place where we go to get our needs met, as a priesthood of believers we go *to meet needs*. If you can grasp this and help others do the same, you'll completely revolutionize the way you do ministry—and the way people's needs are met.

Millions of people wake up every morning, and the first thought they have when their feet hit the floor is, "Do I matter?" We have an incredible opportunity to answer that question in the context of church family. Our churches can touch the lives of people just trying to survive, people who are struggling to succeed, and people striving for significance. The question is: Are we willing to push through objections, make an impact, and help hurting people find answers to their questions?

## OVERCOMING OBJECTIONS

Every person who chooses not to go to church has an excuse that ranges from preachers asking for money too often, to unfriendly people, to busy lives and conflicting activities.

The question we must ask is: What are we doing to eliminate as many barriers as possible so that when visitors do come, they feel welcome? Here's a hint: We started the chapter by talking about this—taking the barriers down starts at the door.

Making people feel welcome involves more than having friendly greeters, but this is the first line against offense. They are the first faces people see, and as the cliché goes, there's no second chance to make a first impression. It isn't enough to be "friendly" because the tendency is to be friendly with people we know—and neglect visitors. We must be outgoing and have our focus on other people and not on ourselves.

When someone enters the building, the clock starts ticking. Surveys show we may have as many as eighteen weeks to disciple new visitors and help them form strong relations and begin to participate. This process starts when we connect with people on their first visit and provide a way for them to hear about the church. The church has a responsibility to communicate its desire and provide activities to meet the needs of the new people, to engage in intentional acts of love and service throughout the week, and to assist new people in finding their place in ministry within this eighteen-week window.

How do you connect people from their first visit and assimilate them into the full life of the church in less than eighteen weeks? By making sure that one of your focus points is discipleship, not just converting the lost. This process allows people to explore *belonging* even before belief or becoming. The sense of family begins when people feel a sense of belonging, but belonging is just the beginning.

People's lives won't change if we "greet" them with scowls of judgment and arms crossed while claiming to represent a Savior who died with His arms wide open. When people come to our churches and feel our love—the love of an entire family welcoming them with an overwhelming sense of belonging—they'll connect with the church just as we have.

# 13 GROW

"We have over-evangelized the world too lightly."[14] Dr. John Perkins used this statement to describe how evangelism becomes counterproductive in a church that isn't practicing discipleship. In many curriculums, conferences, books, and articles, church leaders have embraced an ill-defined discipleship process. Though sincerely motivated, most miss the target and produce inferior results.

Too many people start at the wrong point, which guarantees a wrong result. In theological terms, they're rooted in anthropology (the nature of man) instead of pneumatology (the nature of the Spirit). These models call on the disciple to know rational knowledge (learning, memorization, course work) and do behavioral activity (how to act, what to do).

Knowledge and behavior are essential, but they do *not* transform!

Knowledge stops short of the Holy Spirit's destination of loving God and loving others. Behavioral effort (doing more or behaving better) cancels grace and creates Pharisees.

In too many churches, life in the Spirit is the missing imperative. We must experience the presence and the power of the living God. We need to deconstruct discipleship as it exists today, exchanging rational/behavioral models for relational/experiential models. However, these bold, nearly radical statements are counterintuitive to everything many of us were taught about discipleship.

Let me explain my journey. I serve on a Global Discipleship Task Force commissioned by Empowered 21 and led by a friend and mentor, Dr. David Ferguson. His book *Relational Foundations* introduced the relational model the Task Force has been working on for the past several years. It's been an exciting journey. Dr. Ferguson's teaching and writings and the work of the Discipleship Task Force have inspired this section on discipleship.

## THE RELATIONAL FOUNDATION

Would you recognize a Spirit-empowered disciple if you saw one? Let's explore the rational theology and the behavioral theology I mentioned earlier.

Paul wrote, "All scripture is breathed out by God and profitable for teaching, for reproof, for correction, and for training in righteousness" (2 Tim. 3:16 ESV).

One significant purpose of God's Word is to teach us what we should believe (doctrine). The light of Scripture pierces the darkness of human philosophies and belief systems. Universalism claims there are multiple paths to eternal life, but the light of Scripture declares, "And there is salvation in no one else, for there is no other name under heaven given among men by which we must be saved" (Acts 4:12 ESV).

A second valuable purpose of God's Word is to reveal to us how we should live. Paul said Scripture has been given for reproof (to confront what is wrong) and correction (to define what is right and to equip us to do it). The rebukes of Scripture help us identify areas of darkness while the corrections of Scripture point us toward the light. Paul wrote:

Now the works of the flesh are evident: sexual immorality, impurity, sensuality, idolatry, sorcery, enmity, strife, jealousy, fits of anger, rivalries, dissensions, division, envy, drunkenness, orgies, and things like these. I warn you, as I warned you before, that those who do such things will not inherit the kingdom of God. (Gal. 5:19–21 ESV)

In Ephesians 4:29, Paul speaks of not letting any unwholesome talk come out of your mouth (reproof) but only what is helpful for building others up (correction). To revile, judge, or gossip with our words is to fall outside of the boundary of right living; these are sins.

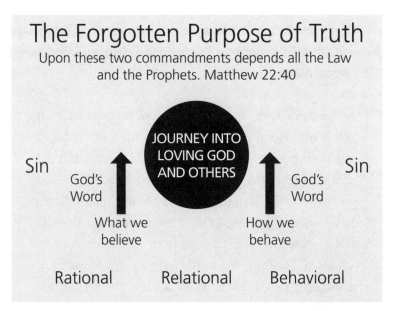

## The Forgotten Purpose of Truth

Upon these two commandments depends all the Law and the Prophets. Matthew 22:40

JOURNEY INTO LOVING GOD AND OTHERS

Sin

God's Word

Sin

God's Word

What we believe

How we behave

Rational          Relational          Behavioral

These two purposes of truth are critical for life and ministry, but they aren't sufficient in themselves. These purposes of truth set boundaries for what we are to believe and how we are to live. God has given these boundaries in order to direct our journey toward a relationship with Him and with those He loves. We might consider these boundaries for doctrine and behavior as the "curbs" alongside our road to intimacy with God. As Paul explains, one of the primary purposes of the law is to be our tutor or our instructor to show us our need for a Savior (Gal. 3:24).

People stand between those two curbs—trying to learn more and trying to behave better. Many end up frustrated, confused, and ineffective as a disciple growing in Christ. Dr. Ferguson observes, "Week by week, they leave church knowing what to believe and how to behave, but never take the journey into a deeper relationship with the God of the Bible."[15] What they need is to take the center path into loving God and loving others revealed in the Great Commandment.

Certainly, Scripture has an objective meaning, but it also has a relational significance. In his book *Relational Discipleship,* Dr. Ferguson explains:

As we have seen, there is a rational purpose of truth and a behavioral purpose of truth, but there is also a relational purpose of truth. In order to understand this relational purpose, we must consider the fourth function of Scripture Paul mentions to Timothy in 2 Timothy 3:16—that of training us in righteousness, or, more literally, "parenting" us. Derived from the Greek word for "children" (*padeia*), the word "training" (*paedeian*) suggests being raised into spiritual maturity by Scripture in a manner similar to being raised by a loving family into physical and emotional maturity.

Scripture has given us the boundaries of right doctrine and right behavior, much like parents give boundaries to their children. But do such boundaries and guidelines—the rules, the "thou shalt nots"—actually raise or mature us? The loving relationships that exist within the boundaries are necessary. A family can have rules, restrictions, and guidelines, but if it lacks love-filled relationships, maturity is hindered. So also it is with our approach to Scripture. Scripture is God-breathed, living, and active, and intended to be experienced in loving relationship with the One who wrote it!

Jesus said that Scripture ("the law and the prophets") hangs, or depends, upon two commandments: Love God, and love others (Matt. 22:35–40). Scripture has a relational purpose: to lead us into maturity through deepened love relationships with the God who breathed it and with those He loves. As the Holy Spirit brings revelation concerning this relational purpose, it seems to "come alive," spurring us to love others, to realize that we are loved, and, above all, to love the One who has given the Word to us.[16]

The core issue of preaching is not "getting something said"; it is not even "getting something heard"; it is "getting something experienced that can transform your life for God and the gospel.[17]

What rational was to the Gutenberg world, experiential is to the Google world.[18]

This Spirit-empowered, relational framework proposes a transforming journey for all ages and stages of spiritual development where the Holy Spirit leads us in a relational journey with God's Son, God's Word, and God's people.

Why is this so important?

I have already mentioned that discipleship deficiencies in the church are alarming. Why do people not live like they say they believe? If what we have been doing is not producing the kind of results (Spirit-empowered disciples) we want, what is wrong?

I do not have all the answers, but I know one of the problems.

"Walk while you have the light, lest darkness overtake you" (John 12:35 ESV).

When we do not walk in the light, we are overtaken by a darkness that blinds our spiritual eyes and we become less faithful, less obedient, and less fruitful. Darkness is always chasing the believer. We must walk in the light.

As mentioned above, there are three sources of light: the Son, the Scriptures, and the Saints. To walk in the light, a person must have a relationship with the sources of light by having:

- **Fresh encounters with Jesus** (John 8:12). "Today you can go into some churches and sit through an entire service and never hear the name of Jesus. The excessive focus on seeker sensitivity, easy ecumenism, empty diversity, political correctness, and cultural atheism have all surreptitiously been planting the seeds of anything goes-ism within our Christian sensibilities."[19] When Jesus taught, His goal was not that everyone would understand Him but that everyone would experience Him. Did anyone encounter Jesus and leave His presence unchanged?

- **Frequent experiences of Scripture** (Psalm 119:105). "The issue of preaching is not getting something said; it is not even getting something heard; it is getting something experienced as a community that can transform lives for God and the gospel."[20]

- **Faithful engagement with God's people** (Matthew 5:14). "Humans are a relational species, and we live in a relational world. In fact this is less an age of information than an age of connection. People are desperate to connect with God, with each other...and with their community. Yet the worlds of the academy and the church remain forums for disseminating 'information' to or at people rather than involving people in the process of connecting with each other in a 'network' of experiences."[21]

Spirit-empowered discipleship requires a lifestyle of the following:

- Fresh encounters with Jesus (John 8:12)
- Frequent experiences of Scripture (Ps. 119:105)
- Faithful engagement with God's people (Matt. 5:14)

The ultimate goal of discipleship is Christ-likeness. Models based upon knowing and doing are incomplete; they lack the empowerment of a life of loving and living intimately with Christ. Spirit-empowered discipleship outcomes must be relational and are impossible to realize apart from the special work of the Spirit. Thus, a Spirit-empowered discipleship outcome, such as *listening to and hearing God,* is relational and requires the Holy Spirit's work.

Relevant discipleship doesn't begin with doctrines or teaching, parables or principles, church polity or stewardship. It begins with loving the Lord with all your heart, mind, soul, and strength. The Spirit calls us to a life of loving intimately and empowers us in it.

As we have freely received, we then freely give. As God gives to us, we give out. When the Holy Spirit is our source, we never have capacity issues.

## AN AGE-STAGE PROCESS

Our first encounter with Jesus, His Word, and His people isn't our last. It's a process. A Spirit-empowered process will produce Spirit-empowered outcomes. Our Task Force has identified forty Spirit-empowered outcomes (listed in the Appendix) and organized them around four main categories:

- Loving the Lord
- Living the Word
- Loving people
- Living God's mission

The goal isn't to live these outcomes only on Sunday but each day of the week. This can't be done without the power of the Holy Spirit. You can't *listen to and hear God* without being tuned into the Spirit of God. You can memorize Bible verses, but you need the power of the Holy Spirit to combat life's pressures and to be a Great Commission and Great Commandment Christian.

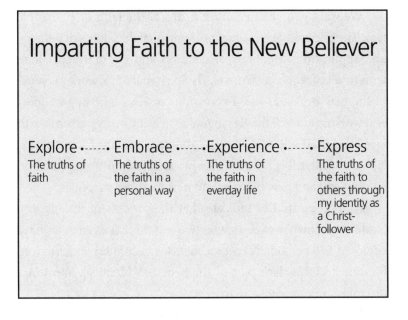

# Imparting Faith to the New Believer

| Explore | Embrace | Experience | Express |
|---|---|---|---|
| The truths of faith | The truths of the faith in a personal way | The truths of the faith in everday life | The truths of the faith to others through my identity as a Christ-follower |

This is the process of faith formation. More than Sunday-only Christianity, it's an everyday walk with Christ.

We want disciples to *explore* truths of the faith in the safety of accepting relationship. This allows belonging before believing. We need to return to God's people experiencing God's Word. These Acts 2 "this is that" moments allow seekers of all ages to explore God's truth in a safe place.

- Accepting people before they change (like Zacchaeus and others) is critical to a safe place for exploring truth.

- Humble, vulnerable servant leaders create safe places to explore God's truths as they share Colossians 3:16-moments of how the Word has dwelled deeply within them.

- Intergenerational times of Spirit-gifted ministry allow exploration of Spirit-empowered living.

We want people to *embrace* truths of the faith in a personal way. The imperative is moments of personal decision, encounters, and application. Moments of decision and commitment along with times of receiving from God's Spirit make His work personal in the new believer's life. Expressions of His Spirit in giftedness and worship allow followers to make their intimacy personal with Jesus and their life in His Spirit. An effective Stage Model of discipleship will inform our approaches to community engagement, evangelism, and new believer and new member strategies.

Numerous studies indicate that the process of discipleship has broken down between stages two and three (i.e., what we have explored and personally embraced hasn't become an experienced lifestyle and thus isn't part of the believer's identity). We desire disciples to *experience* and to *express*.

We want them to *experience* truths of the faith in everyday life—not just on Sunday, but every day of the week. This is where discipleship too often breaks down. It is not just about memorizing Scripture but asking what Bible verses have I experienced today, for instance:

- "Ministering to the Lord with a glad heart" (Ps. 100:2)

- Being still to pray, "Speak Lord, your servant is listening" (1 Sam. 3:8–9)

- Apologizing (confessing) when you have been wrong (James 5:16)

Similarly, we want them to *express* truths to others as Spirit-empowered disciples. An individual like this does these things:

- Listens to and hears God

- Lives life through experiencing Scripture

- Shares His love with those who are near, beginning at home

- Yields to the Spirit for intimacy and discernment, direction, and empowerment

This isn't new. Early church followers used "stage" terms such as seeker, hearer, kneeler, and faithful. (This is based on *The Apostolic Tradition,* written around AD 215 by Hippolytus, Bishop of Rome).[22]

This is effective not only within every stage of our formation but with the developmental process of age maturation. It also works at home.

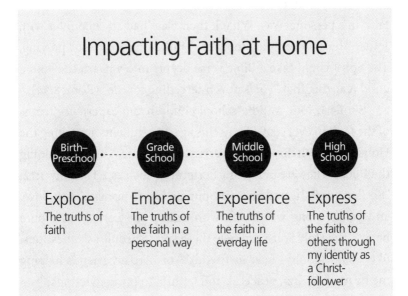

## Impacting Faith at Home

| Birth–Preschool | Grade School | Middle School | High School |
|---|---|---|---|
| **Explore** | **Embrace** | **Experience** | **Express** |
| The truths of faith | The truths of the faith in a personal way | The truths of the faith in everday life | The truths of the faith to others through my identity as a Christ-follower |

## AGE MODEL

Every believer, no matter what age they enter the kingdom of God, begins a process of growing through stages. Similarly, children grow through identifiable stages of human development. We connect these two processes as we produce a discipleship plan for kids to mature in their faith.

We want our preschool children to *explore* truths of the faith in the safety of accepting relationships. This may look like a preschooler leaving Sunday school and a mom asking, "Did you make something in class today?" (This is a common question.) Imagine how thrilled her mom would be when little Amy replies, "'I heard God tell me how to love my brother better!" (This is a relational response.)

Our elementary-school children can *embrace* the truths of the faith in a personal way. What if their class had an encounter with Jesus? The children may meditate on the image of Jesus praying. The Spirit could take a Bible verse deeply into a heart, the young child realizing that "He is now interceding for me" (Rom. 8:34).

Similarly, our middle-school children can *experience* truths of the faith in everyday life. At this age, the students are asking the Holy Spirit to help them experience Scripture—actually "doing the Book." They are practicing Scriptures, such as 2 Timothy 2:22: "So flee youthful passions and pursue righteousness, faith, love, and peace, along with those who call on the Lord from a pure heart." The Holy Spirit can help these young people ask questions, like "Who should I have as friends?" or "Are my friends helping me be more loving, peaceful, and faithful to my convictions?"

As our children mature into young adults, they can *express* truths of the faith to others through their identity as Christ-followers.

## THE LIFESTYLE OF DISCIPLESHIP

Let me repeat, Spirit-empowered discipleship requires a life-style of fresh encounters with Jesus. We must never get too busy working for Him that we lose our relationship with Him. Paul said, "I count all things to be loss in view of the surpassing value of knowing Christ Jesus my Lord" (Phil. 3:8 NASB).

Jesus longs for our praise—praise from those He has blessed, healed, comforted, and encouraged. Picture Him uttering these words: "Where are the other nine" (Luke 17:17 ESV)?

Another way to have a productive encounter with Jesus is to be attentive to His voice—listen to Him. Luke wrote, "Mary . . . sat at the Lord's feet and listened to his teaching" (Luke 10:39 ESV). If we get quiet, we'll hear Him speak. His instructions never mislead us.

Secondly, to be a Spirit-empowered disciple, we need frequent experiences of Scriptures. We can't give out what we haven't received. If we love God, we'll love His Word. It's good to know doctrine and even to memorize the Bible, but it's more important to *practice* the Scriptures daily. That should be our goal.

Peter teaches us, "Since you have in obedience to the truth purified your souls for a sincere love of the brethren, fervently love one another from the heart" (1 Peter 1:22 NASB). Are we practicing that daily? We can practice it by rejoicing with a friend when they have received a great blessing or by comforting a person in their sorrow or by weeping "with those who weep" (Rom. 12:15). This is "doing the Book"!

Anyone who applies the Bible this way is achieving a Spirit-empowered outcome: "Being a living epistle in reverence and awe as His Word becomes real in my life."

Let me say it again: A Spirit-empowered lifestyle requires the fullness of the Spirit. In Ephesians 5:18, Paul says we are to be filled with the Spirit—not a one-time event but a continuous activity. Much of what God requires of disciples can't be done by human effort—and we certainly need the transforming work of the Spirit to change our motives from wanting our own glory to wanting to honor God. We need the supernatural heart and ability provided by the Holy Spirit.

> We must see people as God sees them, or we will never love them as He loves them.

Finally, a Spirit-empowered lifestyle requires faithful engagement with God's people. We must see people as God sees them, or we will never love them as He loves them. We must see people as both fallen and alone. They have spiritual needs as well as relational needs.

My friend, Dr. Ferguson, pointed something out in Scripture that I had never seen before—aloneness actually came before fallenness. In Genesis 2:18, God says that Adam was alone and it was "not good." Several verses *before* Adam and Eve fell into sin (Gen. 3:6), God declared it was not good that Adam was alone. Ferguson observes, "Ministering acceptance and removing a person's aloneness does not mean that we condone sin. Rather, it means that we look deeper in order to see people's needs."[23]

I'm convinced that the path to becoming a Spirit-empowered disciple begins with loving God and loving others, which we can't accomplish without the assistance of the Holy Spirit.

Every church leader needs to ask, "What environments are we creating to allow for powerful, relational connections to occur?" Different churches answer this question in different ways, but churches with effective discipleship always have a clear answer. Many use small groups to encourage heart-to-heart and life-on-life connections. Some have mentoring programs to select and equip rising leaders. Some use Sunday school, classes, seminars, and retreats to bring people together, to deepen relationships, and to impart spiritual truth. Yet these environments aren't enough. Powerful ministries and growing churches always have two additional ingredients in their discipleship process: ministry activities where people apply what they're learning by reaching out to others and a vision to multiply leadership by equipping disciples to disciple others (2 Tim. 2:2). A clear vision for discipleship means that virtually every event is designed to enhance relationships and equip people to love God with all their hearts, serve God gladly and effectively, and multiply themselves in the lives of others.

## MEASURING SPIRITUAL GROWTH

The difficulty of discipleship is that there's an inherent danger in applying any organizational model to the church or to the life of the believer. It's all too easy for the focus to shift from an organic expression of vibrant life and faith to a legalistic list of steps or tasks that can be devoid of the very life we seek to promote.

This doesn't detract from the importance of spiritual disciplines such as prayer, Bible reading, church attendance, witnessing, or stewardship. Followers of Christ throughout the ages have used these and other methods to grow deeper in their walk and fellowship with God. But better questions about spiritual growth focus on whether or not our disciples are exploring, embracing, experiencing, and expressing rather than on how many verses they've memorized. We must ask the right questions if we want to get the right answers.

It's valuable to define certain outcomes for disciples—goals and ideals to aim for. If we fail to set goals, we'll miss them every time. But while Scripture is clear about what a disciple should know (believe) and how a disciple should act (behave), these aren't sufficient and require the added component of relationship, both between believers and between an individual and Christ.

Becoming a better disciple isn't about doing more and knowing more. We can't grade disciples by how many Scriptures they have memorized or use such a principle to define whether one disciple is more spiritually advanced than another. Human effort alone can't produce effective disciples or discipleship outcomes—though it can appear to do so for a time, by some measures. We must have the empowering relationship the Holy Spirit offers each and every believer.

Our goal is to make disciples who make disciples—Spirit-empowered disciples.

Our goal is to make disciples who make disciples—Spirit-empowered disciples.

## FROM INFANTS TO REPRODUCTIVE BELIEVERS

We aren't born again as mature Christians. We're born again as spiritual infants, and through the process of discipleship we grow and mature. In many ways, it mirrors physical growth and maturation.

The way children grow up is so common and predictable we often take it for granted. Many parents simply think they can stand back and watch it happen, and, most of the time, they may be right. Ron Bennett shares in his book *Intentional Disciplemaking* that this wasn't the case for him and his wife, Mary, when they had their first child, Bryan. Shortly after Bryan was born, the doctor informed them that Bryan was having difficulty breathing—it was a problem with the baby's brain.

When Bryan was twenty-five years old, Ron wrote, "Although he has logged about 300 months—9,125 days—on earth, he has never walked, never seen the sun, and never said 'dad' or 'mom'; he has never played baseball, run through a sprinkler, or given us a hug. Immediately after his birth, Bryan became a prisoner in his own body when severe brain damage created multiple handicaps that permanently jammed his maturation process. Consequently, he has 25 years of living but only nine months of normal, healthy development."[24]

Bryan's disability robbed him of the ability to mature, and parents of disabled children everywhere understand the pain that Ron and Mary felt for their son. While they loved him deeply, they couldn't help but wonder what life would have been like if Bryan had developed normally.

I believe that God, our heavenly Father, must have similar feelings when His children get stuck in spiritual infancy. He wants so much more for us than to stay spiritual infants.

When our children are born, it's completely natural for us to do everything for them and to expect very little from them. We dress them and bathe them and feed them. However, we expect our children to grow up and eventually do these things for themselves—that's natural and normal.

Similarly, new believers typically experience an infancy period. We spoon-feed them spiritually and ask very little of them. But just as we don't want to be bathing and dressing our children when they're teenagers, we expect new believers to grow and mature. This happens best through the process of discipleship.

What can we do if we're producing spiritual infants in our churches who never grow and mature spiritually? What do we do if they haven't learned to feed themselves from the Word or to clothe themselves in the righteousness of Christ?

The first step is to evaluate the effectiveness of our discipleship processes. We must honestly ask ourselves if our people are growing spiritually and if we even have the capability of accurately assessing whether we're creating new disciples or simply adding converts. Discipleship spans a continuum from cradle to grave, and we're either advancing or backsliding through that continuum until death. (Remember, if you change the children, you will change the world, and the sooner you start investing, the greater the payoff.)

Be willing to ask hard questions in order to get honest answers of how good a job your church is doing in its discipleship efforts.

I don't believe there is such a thing as discipleship without a systematic study of God's Word. There's no standard without the Bible, there's no target to aim at without the Scriptures, and any teaching that doesn't include the Bible is secondhand information at best. Whether it's delivered in a class, small group, or one-on-one, it's vital to develop a scope and sequence for teaching the meta-narrative of the Bible. The Word is milk for infants and meat for spiritually mature adults, and we should provide both for all ages.

Spoon-feeding the Bible to disciples won't make them mature. They must take personal ownership for studying the Word and learning to "feed" themselves. (My dad used to say, "I don't mind giving you the bottle [of milk], but I get tired of having to part whiskers to get it in your mouth.") We want our people to become wise, and this means we must teach them to study the Bible and rely on the Holy Spirit to guide them.

## DISCIPLESHIP STARTS IN THE NURSERY

Statistics show that adults tend to stop growing spiritually in the fifth to seventh year of their Christian experience. Statistics also show that we need deliberate programs in place for our children, students, and youth. If we don't emphasize discipleship, starting with the nursery—yes, babies!—we are missing an irreplaceable opportunity to help develop lifelong followers of Christ.

When a child goes from children's church to the youth ministries, we should continue building on the foundations created in the earlier years. In many churches, too little consideration is given to connecting children and youth ministries effectively, but this is a vital discipleship step we must not overlook. I can't say enough about the importance of starting young, so it's time to take a critical look at your nursery, children, and youth programs.

Just as you assessed your church earlier, it is time to assess discipleship from the nursery through Sunday school for senior saints. Ask yourself if your church environments are conducive to learning and evaluate the teaching materials you use.

To help you assess your discipleship environments with fresh eyes, pretend you're a visitor and consider what that person might see. Remember, discipleship begins in the nursery, so ask yourself if the signage and system for parents is clear and if there are greeters or other volunteers with good attitudes ready to help them find their way. These things may seem unimportant, but they allow parents and children to have productive, positive experiences, and these issues are magnified in the eyes of new visitors.

Ask yourself similar questions of the discipleship opportunities you have for adults. How would a new believer feel when getting plugged into a class or small group? What can be done to integrate people more smoothly? Who is teaching, and are they operating in their gifts?

Appearance can set the tone and often reflects how much attention we pay to our discipleship programs. Ask yourself if your facility is clean, neat, and painted attractively, creating an environment that promotes learning. Do your nurseries and areas for little ones have new toys or equipment to stimulate these little disciples? Is the church engaging the minds and spirits of older children? Do the youth want to come, or would they rather be somewhere else? What can you do to create a contemporary, stimulating environment with volunteers who can identify with the young people and their unique needs?

While it's helpful to assess the environments for discipleship with fresh eyes, it's perhaps even more important to assess what you are teaching. How long has it been since you reviewed the children's curriculum as a leadership team? You might be surprised to find out how few people know what the church is teaching! Take what you learn in this book and do your best to implement it, not just for adults but to build a foundation of discipleship, evangelism, and worship in children.

We strongly advocate printing or gathering all the church's discipleship materials—kids through adults—and going over them, using what you learn in the Acts 2 process. You can adapt each part of the strategic plan for every stage of discipleship.

Discipleship changes with each phase of life, but the need for it never wanes. Above all, we want people in our churches who become more like Jesus and who minister, serve, disciple, and reproduce the abundant life they enjoy.

## THE PROCESS OF MATURITY

When we consider what it means to be a Christ-follower, we must embrace a holistic approach that focuses on spiritual formation and transformation. Just as we must first be Spirit-empowered if we want to reproduce Spirit-empowered disciples, so we must first be committed to spiritual formation before we promote it to others. Spirit-filled leadership that makes disciples only happens when the Holy Spirit transforms pastors and leaders themselves into disciples.

Spiritual maturity isn't a destination; it's a *process*. It requires time, commitment, and effort to grow spiritually . . . and there are no shortcuts.

When you create empowered disciples, the living and life-giving relationship they have with the Holy Spirit won't let them stay immature; it will urge them forward from glory to glory. They won't be dependent on spiritual leaders to spoon-feed them, correct them, or clean up after them. They'll be mature, Spirit-filled disciples who can accomplish these things any time of the day or night—for the rest of their lives.

This connecting relationship is the key to spiritual growth. When we disciple individuals with a plan of passing on spiritual empowerment, we won't create spiritual children who are dependent on us for every little thing. Instead, we'll help maturing disciples grow and develop into future generations of disciple-makers.

In our work to help leaders develop the five functions in the Acts 2 model of ministry, many have asked a simple but profound question: "What does a Spirit-empowered disciple look like?" In other words, how can church leaders measure spiritual, emotional, and relational growth of individuals, as well as their effectiveness in serving? To answer their question, we've developed a set of "40 Indicators of a Spirit-Empowered Disciple." You'll find this list in the appendix of this book, and you can download a reproducible copy from our website: acts2journey.com

# 14 SERVE

No single factor has greater potential for building a strong, healthy church than mobilizing the congregation to serve God gladly and effectively. Congregation members can go places and do things that their pastors and leaders cannot—even with massive ministries, widely viewed television shows, or dynamic podcasts. Ordinary individuals can reach into the lives of hurting people in unique and powerful ways when they serve inside and beyond the church.

If we could convince the members of our congregations that they are priests, each fulfilling the church's mission, our churches would experience exponential growth. Equipping, training, and developing the laity for ministry is probably the truest demonstration of the Great Commandment and the Great Commission.

God calls every believer and gives every believer gifts and abilities. Our role as church leaders is to help people discover and utilize those gifts—and help them understand they will be held accountable for how they used them.

People who have shifted from consumers to contributors will naturally fulfill a new role, the biblical function we call *serve*. This is an amazing opportunity, both fulfilling a church's normal needs and opening countless doors into our communities—all while furthering the formation of our disciples' spiritual maturity. Nothing helps a churchgoer feel more connected or have a greater sense of ownership than becoming involved in a form of service, and this type of organic service is indispensable when it comes to ministering personally to as many people as possible.

The key to the serve factor is to move away from the leader-helper mentality most churches have and toward a team mentality where the pastor or other leaders become developers rather than the only ones doing ministry.

## IT TAKES A TEAM

Pastors need to equip the saints for the work of the ministry, so developing the next generation of leaders must be a core value component as you determine how the *serve* factor fits your church.

The acronym TEAM can be helpful in this process. Developing a team requires building *trust*, *empowering* team members to make decisions, providing *accountability*, and creating a climate of *mentorship*.

People who are on a team must trust each other, and they do so through consistency of action, loyalty of devotion, and through time. When we each believe we're part of a kingdom of priests who are charged with the Great Commission and the Great Commandment, we realize that we bear a responsibility.

One of the hardest tasks for a pastor can be delegating decisions to Spirit-empowered team members. This is also an issue of trust because we must trust that the disciples we are developing are empowered by the Holy Spirit. When they are, they can go places, think of things, and take Spirit-led initiative that you simply don't have the time or resources to match.

Accountability is incredibly important in this team-building process. I define accountability as offering necessary information before it's required—transparency. I like to explain it like this: For those men who are married, if your wife has to ask you how she looks, it's already too late. You needed to offer that information before she asked for it.

Or it may help to think about it like this: If I walk through the house late at night and my wife hears the garage door open, my car start, and me drive off, she's likely to be put out. If she questions me and I respond defensively, there will be tension in our home. But if I simply offer the information from the onset that I'm heading to the grocery store and will be back in twenty minutes, it's a non-issue.

Mentors and those being mentored are disciples. As we discussed in the previous chapter, you can't build disciples through a Sunday morning service. As leaders, we must invest in the "Timothies" in our lives, pouring into them what we've learned in our own Christian walk.

In addition to communicating the priesthood of all believers, many things go into making dynamic teams. Two of the most basic are having common goals (vision) and engaging in open communication (relationship). It's a sad statistic that only 5 percent of church leaders can state a vision for their church. How can we expect anyone to share a vision if we can't articulate that vision?

First, catch the vision, then cast it—communicate it so your team can buy into it. When you do this, you'll create a powerful, ministering group with far more reach than you could ever have alone.

Let me provide some additional insights and direction:

- **Enlist**—Cast a clear, compelling vision. Personally interview the person and show the benefits and blessings of serving, not the burden of having to serve.

- **Expectations**—Explain what is expected of someone serving in a particular role, such as in the sound booth or as a parking lot greeter. To quote an old adage: You can't inspect what you haven't expected.

- **Equip**—Give a scriptural foundation for the role (biblical examples of service), provide adequate resources, and make sure volunteers will function in their gifting and ability.

- **Engage**—Actually release them with responsibility and trust them with some level of authority.

- **Evaluate**—Review expectations and evaluate performance. This is where accountability comes in.

- **Encourage**—Remember that these are volunteers. Praise them in public; correct them in private.

## WHY DID JESUS COME?

When we think of why Jesus came to earth, we can make a list that includes saving people from their sins, healing the sick, giving hope to the hopeless, and a host of other ministries. In everything He said and did, Jesus served others. Someday, He will return as the conquering King, but He first came as a humble servant. Jesus told His disciples, "But whoever desires to become great among you, let him be your servant. And whoever desires to be first among you, let him be your slave—just as the Son of Man did not come to be served, but to serve, and to give His life a ransom for many" (Matt. 20:26–28).

We can easily gloss over this as nice-sounding rhetoric, but stop and think about the fact that God's Son, the Word made flesh, came down from heaven as a helpless baby, grew up as the son of a carpenter, and dedicated His earthly ministry not to glorifying

Himself but to bringing glory to His Father by serving sheep with no shepherd.

This is more than just a leadership model; serving is a way of life, the foundation of the gospel. Jesus did more than talk about it—He lived it. Perhaps one of the greatest demonstrations of servant-heartedness was when Jesus washed His disciples' feet (John 13).

Again, don't simply think you know this story and gloss over it. Stop, forget what you've heard or read before, and see it with fresh eyes. The Creator of the universe put aside His glory, wrapped a towel around Himself, and took the position of the lowest servant.

For a moment, consider what people in the ancient Middle East would have walked through in their sandaled feet. Think about what was on the streets, what the animals left behind, what was clogging the gutters. There was no sewage system, and people didn't drive around in nice, neat cars but walked dirt roads with dung-dropping animals everywhere. Think of the heat and the sweat that dripped down a Middle Eastern man's legs, cutting runnels through the dirt caked to his skin.

This is what Jesus washed off their feet—animal dung and human waste and dust and dirt and sweat and grime. It would quickly have made the bowl of water brown and revolting!

This wasn't merely a symbolic gesture. It was a status quo-destroying demonstration of the selfless heart of a true servant.

It was the example Jesus gave to His disciples as one of His final acts on this earth. "Do you know what I have done to you?" Jesus asked them. "You call Me Teacher and Lord, and you say well, for so I am. If I then, your Lord and Teacher, have washed your feet, you also ought to wash one another's feet. For I have given you an example, that you should do as I have done to you.

. . . If you know these things, blessed are you if you do them" (John 13:12–17).

If Jesus did this for His disciples, including Judas who would shortly betray Him, how can we ignore the precedent He set for us? How can we not strive to mimic this servant-heartedness to those we disciple by serving them sacrificially?

Further, what would happen in any church if most of the churchgoers caught on to this? How might they serve one another? What needs would we meet if we served as God's hands and feet?

Jesus wasn't just serving His disciples; His purpose wasn't just that they would have clean feet. His purpose was to develop them into the future leaders of the church, who would in turn equip the saints for ministry and teach them to do the same.

We should be no different.

## FINDING PURPOSE

Earlier in the book, I talked about purpose and how important it is to help those we disciple to discover the reason God put them on earth. Serving is directly related to purpose, and God has given us spiritual gifts and talents to use them for His glory and to accomplish our purpose. Your gifts, natural abilities, and personality form a composite—a unique combination that is as specific to you as your fingerprint. It's the way God wired you, and it makes you qualified for the calling He puts on your life.

Generally, we see three different categories of gifts in the Bible. The first are *manifestation gifts*, drawn out of 1 Corinthians (most Pentecostals and charismatics typically think of these when we say "gifts"). Next are *ministry gifts*, found in Ephesians 4. Finally, we have *motive gifts* in Romans 12, which we can sometimes overlook because they're similar to natural abilities.

Some of these gifts tend to operate more in a corporate sense than within individuals. We would probably say that the gift of healing operates in our church rather than in the life of an individual, who may exercise a gift but may not always possess it.

Each individual has spiritual gifts, natural abilities, distinct passions, and unique life experiences, all of which go into creating their personality, view of the world, and ability to accomplish their God-given purpose. Helping congregants discover their spiritual gifts can open doors they never knew existed and may help them discover untapped potential and opportunities for service. There are many spiritual-gift tests and programs for discovering them (we'll discuss this later), and this can be an excellent means of discipleship formation.

Operating within your gifts and natural abilities is like writing with your dominant hand. Have you ever broken or injured your dominant hand and had to write with your other hand? It takes much longer, and it never looks quite right. It's uncomfortable. Something similar happens when people serve in an area that isn't in line with their gifts. One of our goals is to help volunteers find where they can serve most comfortably and effectively.

> Operating within your gifts and natural abilities is like writing with your dominant hand.

That's doesn't mean we aren't obligated to forms of service that are mundane simply because we aren't "gifted" in that area. There isn't a chance in the world that Jesus would have listed "feet washing" on His spiritual-gift test! Yet He was a servant of all and demonstrated clearly that the most humbling acts of service are befitting for even the highest leader. I try never to ask someone to do something that I'm not willing to do or have not done personally.

One church I know of had the policy that any pastor who wished to serve had to first work on the janitorial staff as a "green shirt." There are few things more basic than serving a congregation by cleaning the restrooms after services, and I imagine it gave the ministry staff a unique perspective on Jesus' foot washing ministry!

So while we serve to meet church needs—regardless of whether or not we're "gifted" to change diapers, welcome visitors, or help with the youth—we want to help people find their fit and serve out of their gifts. We want people who can carry a tune to sing in the worship team, people who are friendly to welcome others at the door, and trustworthy individuals to usher and collect our offerings.

## HUMBLE ORIGINS, AMAZING SERVICE

We can enrich lives and open amazing doors of service by helping people understand their natural abilities and how these abilities complement their personalities, connect with their passions, and fit in the context of their life experiences. We can use assessment tools, books, and small-group settings to help develop these points in our discipleship programs, but again, our example in this is Christ, who made Himself a servant of all.

It can also be helpful to think of people throughout the Bible who had great destinies but started off in lowly positions. David's father didn't even bring him in from the fields when the prophet Samuel came and asked to see his sons. As the youngest, David was an afterthought, relegated to the lowly duties of being a shepherd. This wasn't a noble calling; it was some of the lowest work, reserved for servants. David wasn't low man on the totem pole; he was left off the pole entirely!

Yet God saw much more in David than anyone else possibly could, and those times of menial labor with stupid, smelly sheep proved to be the foundation of a poet's soul in a warrior's body. David was Israel's greatest king, but he got his start as a lowly servant.

Gideon is also an excellent example. Hiding in a depression in the ground and doing manual labor, this fearful son of an unimportant man found God prophetically calling him a mighty warrior! God saw something in Gideon no one could see from his hidden workplace—a willing tool for bringing victory to His people.

Does that describe us? Is that an accurate view of our own ego and opinion of ourselves? Are we content to let God call us out of a hidden threshing floor and use us as His tool? Or do we seek to promote ourselves?

No discussion of service can happen without a right understanding of humility because without humility as a foundation stone, successful service can go to our heads. This is as true of any congregation member as it is of those in leadership, but we bear an extra burden not only to maintain humble hearts ourselves but to reproduce humility in those we disciple.

A friend tells an amusing anecdote of praising one of the parking lot attendants at his church and creating a joking title of "Captain Parking Lot Attendant." The next week, the man showed up with a ridiculously bright flashlight, a garish sports coat, and a hat befitting a cruise line captain. He looked ridiculous—and provided his pastor an uncomfortable opportunity to explain the importance of humility in serving.

We don't want anyone to be Captain Parking Lot Attendant. Don't let successful service go to your head, and train those you disciple to minister in humility and keep the right opinion of themselves as they serve.

## SERVICE TOOLS

Spiritual-gift assessments help individuals discover their gifts, but the assessment also benefits church leaders. When we help others discover their spiritual gifts and natural talents, we're investing in the most important resources within the church. I encourage church leaders to sow into their ministry staff and lay leaders in the congregation by helping them explore their spiritual gifts.

Assessment tools provide an inventory of the spiritual resources each individual can contribute to the body, and it's empowering to help people see which gifts are most evident in their life experiences, current ministry efforts, and possible future church involvement. When people understand their gifts, it helps us fit them into ministry opportunities more confidently. It also helps us as leaders locate the right people to meet various needs within the body.

Assessment tools and surveys help to identify a person's gifts and abilities, but these tools aren't the complete answer. These instruments may be an accurate reflection of a person's desire to serve God in a particular role, but the person may or may not have the God-given ability to serve effectively in that role. As we help people find their proper place in a role that inspires them and expands God's kingdom, we need to encourage them to try different ministry opportunities to see

> When we help others discover their spiritual gifts and natural talents, we're investing in the most important resources within the church.

where they thrive and excel. Let me offer another insight about the gifts: The Holy Spirit can take the improbable, unlikely, and least qualified people among us and use them in unimaginable ways. The Bible is filled with stories of unlikely candidates whom God used in extraordinary ways. Moses stuttered, Elijah got burned out and was fearful of Jezebel, Jeremiah was depressed, Thomas doubted, Paul was a murderer, and Peter had a short fuse. I could go on, but you get the point. The Holy Spirit can trump any flaw, disability, or inadequacy.

I've found that the best way to help people find their place of ministry is to teach about spiritual gifts and lead people in a discovery activity. At the same time, trust your observations and depend on the Holy Spirit to guide.

Every congregation has a variety of ministry needs within the church and the community. As you learn the gifts and natural talents of your ministry staff and volunteers, you can help them get plugged into areas where they can use those gifts most effectively.

Perfection isn't the goal here. While we want to help people serve in areas that are most aligned with their gifts, simply getting people involved and then fine-tuning their areas of service can help congregants contribute to the body of Christ and take ownership of the church and its various ministries.

A friend of mine likes to tell the story of a woman who had been teaching Sunday school for more than twenty years. He was a relatively new pastor at the church and after delivering a message on spiritual gifts, this woman came up to him and told him that although she had been teaching Sunday school for twenty-one years, it wasn't really her gift. Apparently, that was obvious, and the joke was that she had gotten stuck teaching Sunday school by walking too slowly in the hallway one day and letting the pastor at that time catch up with her. He had asked for a few weeks of help, and twenty-one years later she was still doing what he had asked her to do—not because it was her gift but because she was willing.

They were probably the longest "few weeks" of her life!

As they talked, it became obvious to my friend that she had gifts of hospitality, and he promised that in two weeks, he would find someone to take over her class so she could join the greeter team. Her eyes lit up! Everything began to change for her as she stepped into the role that fit her gifts, and God used her in incredible ways once she got to the right place.

Many people are serving in our churches because they're trying to be helpful, which is commendable. But how much more effective would they be if we took the time to help them learn their gifts and place them in areas of service where they could excel?

Our churches are full of people who didn't think they could serve or succeed in a certain capacity until someone believed in them. As leaders, that's our job—to see people as God's masterpieces and encourage them to use the gifts He has given them. Every person has talents they can use for God's glory and their own fulfillment.

> Every person has talents they can use for God's glory and their own fulfillment.

Sometimes we may see a person's gifts before they do. A friend tells a story of the need for a Sunday school teacher for a class of junior girls. After exhausting a list of the parents whose girls were that age, the volunteer leader told my friend that someone had been on his mind to lead the class. This young woman was still in high school, and there was no obvious indication that she had a teacher's gifts. She was just a quiet, sweet-spirited girl—a bit of a wallflower.

The volunteer leader decided to invite her to become the teacher for that class, and over the next several months and years she became one of the best teachers that church had ever seen. Young girls flocked to her, and she had an enormous impact on many lives! To the natural eye, she didn't seem a good fit to teach, but the Spirit prompted this leader to help her uncover her gifts by putting her in the right place to exercise them.

Often times people only need someone to believe in them and give them a chance to use their God-given gifts and abilities. Instead of simply taking advantage of a willing person, like the Sunday school teacher who served twenty-one years, the Holy Spirit's inspiration can help us mine untapped potential in the people around us.

The point isn't just to staff various church programs with gifted and talented individuals but to help disciples grow and develop by serving in ways that benefit both the body as a whole and the individual as a maturing believer.

When you begin to emphasize serving, there can be a down side, as well. Some people will get involved and prove to be ineffective. When I recruited people, I frequently put a sunset on their initial time of involvement. I might ask for a six-month commitment with an evaluation at the end of that time. If everything went well and they wanted to stay in the position, it would continue. If not, we would begin an exit strategy. Although it may be risky, releasing people to serve is well worth it.

It only takes one person serving to change a life, but in God's economy, the math works a little differently. A lost person may come to Christ because one person volunteered to serve. An individual has been saved, but the life of the volunteer has changed as well—and so do the lives of all who are blessed when the new believer grows and matures by serving God and glorifying Him. The ripple effect of God's blessing, power, and love is endless.

We serve a God of multiplication!

# 15 GO

Jay Martin was serving as a pre-sentence and probation officer for a circuit judge while he attended law school in Little Rock, Arkansas. As he performed his duties, he was overwhelmed by the number of African-American males he saw coming through the court. One of his duties was to record these individuals' stories, and he began to notice common characteristics: single-mother households, drug charges, poverty.

Jay wondered, *What might change if someone intervened earlier in their lives?* Could some be spared a future of crime if someone simply loved enough to care? Jay had come from a broken home himself, and he began to feel troubled by the young men who came through the court.

One day he went to lunch with the head probation officer, but they didn't go to the hottest foodie destination in suburbia. Instead, they went to one of the impoverished areas where many of the people they saw in court came from. As they returned from lunch, they passed through an area that was boarded up and had all kinds of graffiti on the walls.

Jay asked the probation officer what that part of town was called. He gave him a knowing look and replied simply, "The projects."

God put a desire to return to this area on Jay's heart, and when the boarded-up areas reopened, he began to head there on Saturday mornings to play basketball. He went first in the spring of 1998—alone. That first day, he played basketball with one eight-year-old boy. He returned to play basketball every Saturday, slowly earning the trust of the boys who came to play.

Eventually, Jay left his position as a college and career ministry director for First Assembly of God in North Little Rock in order to focus his ministry attention on this area. He's still there today, having logged more than seventeen years of ministry in the Amelia B. Ives housing project.

While Jay started the work alone, he didn't remain alone. First Assembly bought property and later added a more worship-friendly sanctuary, naming the church Metro Worship Center. Inspired by Matthew Barnett and the Los Angeles Dream Center, Metro began a homeless ministry. They bussed in homeless people from rescue missions for a 5:30 p.m. worship service—at which Jay preached. Hot on the heels of this worship service, they bussed in students from the ten most challenged neighborhoods in Little Rock for ROCK Kids Ministry and Revolution Student Ministry.

Their efforts have inspired children, poverty-stricken families, and homeless people to become lifelong followers of Jesus Christ. Metro is passionate about building a bridge of relationship from the hearts of the displaced, desperate, and unchurched people of Little Rock to the heart of Jesus.

Additional ministries and events have caught on, including Camp Love, which they hold every summer, and an annual Thanksgiving dinner buffet, which takes over the city fairgrounds. City leaders have embraced Metro's efforts, disregarding party lines in their support, and those political opportunities have opened doors for Jay personally. As an evangelical Christian, pro-family, small-government guy, he was elected to the state legislature and later asked to serve as Majority Leader.

All the things God has done through this man's willingness to go into the poorest areas of Little Rock could take up an entire chapter and more, but the point isn't to glorify Jay. The opposite is true: Jay's willingness and efforts to serve others glorify *God*! The point is that Jay is just an ordinary guy who was willing to go where God sent him. He could have been anyone.

Any willing disciple of God can change the world, but we must go out into that world in order to make a difference.

## THE FUTURE HANGS IN THE BALANCE

The future of the church hangs in the balance, and *go* is one of the most central factors in how that future will come together. Will we stay relevant, or will the church's influence wane until it is impotent?

Leaders long for their churches to grow, for people to experience the transforming love of Jesus, for families to be healed, and for communities to enjoy reconciliation, but many of these leaders are perplexed by the lack of spiritual vitality. What's the problem? A church, like anything else, goes through stages. A new church plant has new members who grow through spiritual phases as the church grows. From birth to infancy to childhood to adolescence, believers grow like children—and with them, the church grows.

Mature believers are in their prime and should be creating disciples, using their growth and maturation to foster younger believers. The

> Mature Christians should help raise other growing, maturing Christians.

process should be beginning again and again in a constant flow of renewal: Mature Christians should help raise other growing, maturing Christians.

Unlike people who grow old and eventually die, organizations have the capacity to reinvigorate themselves, to instill new energy and vitality, and to keep growing through countless stages. Unfortunately, organizations can also be like people, becoming stiff with age, looking backward instead of forward, and failing to find new sources of vitality for new growth. Once an organization reaches its prime it may plateau and experience declining growth. If the decline isn't arrested and reversed, the organization can die.

We sometimes see this happen in congregations in which the members' average ages are far older than the communities they serve. The congregation stagnates at some point, and too few new people came in to refresh the church with a new vision.

I believe the key they often miss is the process we call *go*, which changes the inward focus into an outward focus.

Every church needs new life, and since we can't stop or turn back the aging process of the people who attend the church, the only way to seed new life into the church is through new people and new vision.

Though there are exceptions, most churches don't experience a regular flow of guests without being intentional about going out and inviting them to come. As new people become a part of the congregation, the church must invest in them and empower them. Churches that don't redirect resources to new ministries will typically lose the new people upon whom their future depends.

The unchurched would like to develop a real and sincere relationship with a Christian. Over 17 million people would accept Christ if presented with the gospel. Another 43 million are close. Dr. Thom Rainer pulls no punches when he writes, "I am convinced that the answer to all the troubling questions about the church in America is very simple. We Christians have become disobedient and lazy. Investing our lives in the lives of lost and unchurched people is inconvenient and messy. The silence of Christians may be one of the greatest tragedies in the church today."[25]

## RELATIONAL EVANGELISM

So what's the secret? More short-term missions? Long-term missions? The answer is simple—and yet difficult. While worldwide missions is a core component of *go*, many churches have seemingly chosen evangelistic complacency or missions work in other continents over the most needed and effective means of going into all the world: relational evangelism. We don't need one or the other; we need both!

We need to understand what relational evangelism means, what it looks like, and how we do it. We're often willing to do secondhand evangelism, which means we'll talk to anybody about Jesus as long as we don't have to see them again, but we're hesitant to share Christ with people we will see again. We're willing to travel overseas or go downtown and hand out tracts or talk to people because once we leave those environments, chances are we'll never see those people again. Our neighbors are another story.

Too many of us aren't willing to share with those nearest to us because we'll see those people again and could be embarrassed. In addition, we aren't willing to build relationships with people before we witness to them. We want to witness on the front end of a relationship, while effective witness has to come on the back end.

We must be willing to share Jesus in the context of relationship, and this is a new paradigm for many. Ninety-five percent of churches have never understood how to do this, although the statistics indicate that 99 percent of all people who know Jesus are saved because someone personally reached out to them. Yet we still ignore these facts, thinking that we can reach the lost without getting personally involved with the lost.

We want to share Jesus without risk, without getting "dirty." We want to send money around the world for others to do it for us, and some of us will even go ourselves if there are no strings attached and we can walk away without a great deal of personal risk. Witnessing to our neighbors or coworkers is a completely different dynamic because it's risky and it requires that we be responsible for our daily actions.

> We must recognize that we have to earn the right to share Jesus before we can share Him.

Developing relationships with the lost before sharing the good news with them is a big shift. We must recognize that we have to earn the right to share Jesus before we can share Him.

This shift goes hand-in-hand with the concept of the priesthood of all believers, because our churches aren't going to grow by sending missionaries overseas. They're going to grow when our people learn that it's their responsibility to invite guests from their daily life to church.

Part of the problem is that we've taught our people to stay away from the world. This hothouse mentality makes us want to spend all our time with other Christians so we won't be tainted by the people of the world. We've adopted a defensive posture instead of an offensive posture, partly out of this hothouse mentality and partly because we're afraid to offend—and be rejected.

We say the presence of God is manifested when we come together in church, but we've forgotten that we are the temples of the living God—we take His presence with us everywhere we go. His presence isn't limited to the church building. When we walk into an office building full of unchurched people, we have brought the presence of God into that place.

*Buildings* can't tell people about Jesus. He isn't in a building. He's with His priests—each and every one of us who bears His name.

## ENGINES FOR NEW LIFE

Does this mean evangelism doesn't or shouldn't happen in church buildings? No, of course not—it simply means that too many people who sit inside the building expect the unsaved to come into the building, where the pastor will do the work of evangelism.

Membership surveys testify to the importance of lay ministry. Nearly 70 percent of first-time attendees come to church as a result of a personal invitation. Think what would happen if everyone in your church invited someone next Sunday. Dr. Thom Rainer's research reports that "82 percent of the unchurched are at least 'somewhat likely' to attend church if they were invited. Only 21 percent of active churchgoers invite anyone to church in the course of a year. Only 2 percent of church members invite an unchurched person to church."[26]

Strategic plans to bring people into church are only as effective as our efforts to tackle the problem of relational evangelism. Without this, programs and initiatives are missing the point.

While this doesn't mean that we shouldn't devise efforts to bring the unsaved into our churches, it does mean that the burden of ministry doesn't belong to the pastor; it belongs to each and every believer. When the people in your church grasp this paradigm shift, you can begin to implement methods of making your meetings a warm and welcoming place for believers to minister the gospel.

We call the efforts that most successfully draw new people into the church building "engines." The most effective methods of bringing in new people fall into three categories: friends, neighbors, and strengths.

First, look to your friends. The best place to find the unsaved is among the people your congregation members already connect with every day. Successful, growing churches have many people—not just the ministry staff—who own this responsibility and invite their friends to church. As we mentioned previously, many people want to come to church but are simply waiting for an invitation.

> We must help our congregations understand that attracting new people is not the pastor's job.

We must help our congregations understand that attracting new people is *not* the pastor's job. Pastors aren't paid to reach new people; they're paid to shepherd those who come. That doesn't mean that pastors can't reach the lost as well. If we're going to see people in the pews become more engaged in evangelism, we must share stories of how *we* are engaging non-Christians.

A church leader in Canada made some statements I love. He asked his pastors to give the names of five non-Christians they were talking to, interacting with, and establishing relationships with. Then he said, "We can either lead from the pulpit or from the streets."

It's our job as pastors and leaders to teach and disciple the people in our churches, equipping them for ministry. We must convey to each one that as believers they have a mandate to go into their worlds and make relationships with the hurting, the oppressed, and the sick so they may be helped and healed. Remember this: The building isn't the church; the people inside the building are the church.

There are many ways to make it easier for congregants to invite their friends, including special events and hospitality initiatives. In the end, however, it comes down to having relational evangelism as a core value and an active, intentional part of your church's DNA.

The second engine is identifying your church's "neighbors." When you look for people to love, why not look "next door"? Plenty of people are your geographical neighbors; they drive or walk by your church every day.

Don't limit your thinking to blitzing neighborhoods and going door to door. Serving the community is a powerful testimony to those who need to know God. James admonished us to show people our faith by our works, and working in the community to draw in neighbors can be an excellent way to touch the lives of individuals who desperately need God.

This relates to the third engine, which is to look to your church's ministry strengths for ways to connect with new people. Every church has unique strengths, though some may not be obvious. Ask your ministry staff and trusted congregants what your church does well, and then do it extremely well in the context of reaching un-churched and under-churched people.

If your church excels at ministering with music, you might set up concerts in local parks. Grill some burgers and hot dogs, hand out cold drinks, and play excellent music. Play some songs everybody knows, and then introduce some God-focused worship music. You can revolutionize warm summer nights with a few good tunes and a cool drink.

Perhaps your church has a group of creative people. Get them busy with art shows or videos or web-based platforms that will attract other people as cool and creative as they are! There's no end to the creative things people can generate when the assignment is to make new friends.

Your church may have men who like to repair cars. Consider having a single mothers' day where moms can get help maintaining and repairing their cars. While the men work on the cars, women can offer the moms a place where their kids can play while they enjoy a cup of coffee or tea and a chat with other moms from your church. Discover the needs of these single moms and determine what your church can do to help them.

Most of all, we must encourage the people in our churches not to be so afraid of rejection that they avoid engaging with people personally and relationally, for that's where real ministry happens.

## USE YOUR STRENGTHS, WHATEVER THEY ARE

One of our Acts 2 Journey facilitators tells the story of brainstorming with a room full of pastors and their dream teams about the strengths of their churches. He noticed that one small church wasn't fully participating in the discussion, and, eventually, he had heard from every church except this one. The pastor was in his early sixties, and everyone in the leadership group was in that age bracket or beyond. Finally, he addressed them directly: "What about you guys? What are you good at?"

They were silent for a little while, and the facilitator began to feel bad for singling them out, but after a short delay, the pastor's wife blurted out, "Funerals!"

Everyone in the room laughed good-naturedly, and the facilitator asked what she meant.

"Well," she said, "when we have a funeral, our ladies do an incredible funeral dinner. The food they prepare for the family is amazing! And though a lot of our men don't have suits, they come dressed in the best clothes they have got and do a great job of being gracious and caring for the family as they grieve." She looked over at her husband, perhaps deciding whether or not to go on, and said, "My husband is a good preacher on Sunday, but he's an amazing preacher at funerals!"

Her husband slumped down in his chair a little bit, embarrassed that funerals were his best strength, but he nodded his head like he knew it was true. Before the facilitator could say anything more, the pastor's wife said, "I know what we can do! We can call the local funeral home and tell them that anytime a grieving family doesn't have a church to help with the funeral, *we* can do it! That can be our outreach! Our ladies can cook the meal, our guys can usher, and my husband can preach an amazing service and minister to those hurting people."

It turns out the local funeral home did perhaps a dozen such funerals a year, and this church was able to help families in this way about once a month. They walked out of the room excited to have a strategy that used their strengths to go outside the walls of their church and gave them a vital outward focus.

## FOOD SERVICE

Maybe your church's strength isn't funerals, but you have a strength. Don't let size intimidate you. You can have a high-impact church even in a small community because the principles God built the church upon are not about size. I love hearing stories about how individuals and churches are making impacts on their communities and seeing people saved, because *go* isn't limited to big churches with big budgets.

Dave Campbell pastors a small church in Timbo, Arkansas, a town that has fewer than 100 inhabitants. The last time I visited the church, 117 people were present for a service, but what I love about them has nothing to do with numbers. While their church routinely gives sacrificially to missions, they have a passion for relational evangelism and outward focus that I find truly inspiring.

A tornado once ripped through their tiny town and knocked out the power there and in the adjacent, larger town of Mountain View. The storm devastated these communities, leaving many people homeless and struggling to clean up the debris, to get the power running, or even to cook a meal.

Just four days after the tornado, Dave and a few of the men from his church headed over to Mountain View to see what they could do to help. They arrived just as a disaster relief team was packing up their station in a local grocery store's parking lot. When Dave asked why they were leaving when the needs were just coming in, the relief worker told him, "We're just disaster relief. We can stay four days, and then we're gone."

Dave and his men looked at the needs of that community and decided they would do what they could to help. They pulled an old smoker over to the parking lot, and he and his guys started cooking food. Someone gave them a grill, and the grocery store gave them produce they couldn't sell anymore because they couldn't keep it refrigerated. Dave and his men fed so many people they were cooking long after midnight. If someone arrived and was hungry, they got up and cooked food—any time, day or night.

Dave put out a cot and slept in that parking lot for six days and nights, serving roughly 1,500 meals a day and being available twenty-four hours a day. He told me that some days they didn't know where the food would come from, but as they ran out, people would bring more food from their powerless freezers. They cooked everything from salmon to hot dogs; whatever people brought, they cooked.

As Dave and his team served the people of Mountain View, others began to volunteer, and the food ministry created amazing relationships between the people of these communities, Dave, and the church. It gave them unparalleled access to people who would normally never set foot inside a church, including the meth makers who came out of the wooded hills for help.

God got a hold of one of these men who had run a methamphetamine lab up in the hills. He got saved and exchanged running a meth lab for running a prison ministry, reaching out to the people who used to buy drugs from him.

Dave watched God not only show His goodness and love to the people of those rural towns as he and his men fed them and helped them in practical ways—Dave's church also saw the impact of all those touched lives.

A pastor friend of Dave's, Bob Caldwell, shared with me what God was doing in his community as well. Eleven years before we spoke, God had impressed a Scripture on him: Matthew 25 is where Jesus says that when He was hungry and thirsty and naked, some fed and clothed Him while others did not.

At the time, Bob's church had only a few families in it, but he challenged them each to give a dollar a day for a month so they could start a food bank ministry. He had thirty people each give a dollar a day, starting their food bank with $900. Because it was such a tight-knit community, a local Baptist church gave them another $500, and with these funds, they began feeding people. Over the years, they experienced problems because they had to learn how to run a food ministry, but it survived. Three years after they started, Diane Sawyer brought a film crew from ABC to do a story on how they were feeding 2,000 a month—in a town of 400 people.

Bob now has thirty other outlets like the one that began in his church, and they feed 8,000 people a month who would otherwise go hungry. Because of their work in the community and the trust and relationship it has fostered, his church plans to start multiple services.

Bob's son, Josh, was preaching in a surrounding town when a young man named Bubba walked up to him and said, "I've only met one other Caldwell in my life. When I was nine-years-old, he walked up to our porch to see my daddy and gave him a box of food. Do you know that guy?"

"That was my dad," Josh replied.

Bubba then shared the story about how Pastor Caldwell first met his family. One day, a man showed up at their door—a preacher, inviting them to church. "My name is Brother Caldwell," he introduced himself, "and I would love to invite you to visit our church next Sunday."

Bubba said his father, James, wasn't receptive to the invitation. He said, "Don't bother us! I know you're just trying to do your job by inviting us to church, but I'm not interested. Me and the 'Man Upstairs' don't have a good relationship. I'm not interested. Don't bother me anymore."

As the pastor was leaving, he noticed they were all eating popcorn. He said to James, "It's a little early to be eating a snack, isn't it?" My dad replied, "It's not a snack. This is what I've been feeding my family for the last three weeks." Brother Caldwell left and told his wife about the incident. They were so moved by the needs of this family that they took their grocery money and bought a box of food to take back to the family. When they knocked on the door, James came to the door and said, "I told you not to bother me anymore." Pastor Caldwell said, "I saw that you didn't have much to eat. My wife and I decided that if my kids had something to eat, we wanted your kids to have something, as well. If you'll accept this box of food, you may have it." At that moment, my daddy started crying and said, "What time does church start tomorrow morning?" They attended for the next two Sundays, and on the second Sunday, the entire family came to the altar and got saved.

I love this story because we can easily get preoccupied with visions of well-developed ministries, but hearing how a food ministry like Bob Caldwell's got started should remind us of the smaller things we can do to show Christ's love to a needy world. The nature of the call on Bob's life didn't change—he's still feeding people—but it began with small, humble actions like this one.

Your church and your vision don't have to be big for your actions to have a big impact on the people around you.

We can't just wait for people to come into our churches to meet Jesus; we must go out and show Him to them.

## OPEN DOORS FOR THE TRUTH

Each church has strengths. There's something your church can do to turn your focus outward, whether it's having funerals or cooking food. Concerts, rallies, food and clothing drives, and other special outreach events are all amazing ways to connect with new people.

So is teaching the truth! So, how do you get new people to want to listen to the truth? It's simple: meet their needs.

Marriage and parenting events offer valuable help to struggling families. Many people have never seen a good model to emulate and have never heard about marriage and rearing children from a biblical perspective.

Finance seminars can bring wisdom to a debt-laden community. Counseling ministries can offer hope when life has grown bigger than people can manage. If your church is in an ethnically diverse community, classes that teach English can help uplift and empower people. Recovery groups for the addicted or abused can make your church a place of hope for hurting people.

Many churches with excellent teachers limit their gifts to the congregation. Some Sunday school teachers or children's ministers may never use their ministry gifts outside the building, so we must help them take their gifts outside the four walls of the church. Leaders within the church can make excellent mentors, such as at the local YMCA, by volunteering with kids' sports camps. Elementary schools need classroom helpers, and parents can always use a safe, wholesome place for their kids to go for a "parents' night out." When you invest in the kids, you invest in the future in more ways than church attendance.

The list of opportunities is endless and only limited by your imagination! When you serve others, you'll find new friends— and these new people will be the life of your church in the future.

## THE GOAL

The goal in all of this is to extend love and friendship to those outside the church—to build relationships! The point is to use our strengths, geographic location, and friendship circles to make friends and connections. Every church has some combination of these, even churches who are "only good at funerals"!

Don't let excuses keep you from exploring your opportunities. An aging congregation may have lost the energy for community service and may not engage in the most modern music or technology, but they may find they are better at loving than anyone else. As parents and grandparents, they've had the most practice and have seen most of the hardships life has to offer, so they can offer great empathy and godly wisdom.

Every church has at the least one outstanding strength.

Remember that people came to Jesus because of His power to heal, His accessible teaching, and His love and compassion. For these reasons and many more, people came *running* to Jesus—and they still do. We must look for ways to empower, teach, disciple, and show love and compassion to people who need to see Jesus in our lives. But they won't see Him if we don't go to them!

If we'll look carefully at our churches, we'll discover a unique evangelism DNA for each one. When we do, we must aim at the target: people outside our doors. We can waste a lot of energy trying to fix our weaknesses, which is exhausting and frustrating. But when we pour our best efforts into our strengths, we'll find energy we didn't know we had.

An aging church isn't destined to pass out of relevance; it simply needs to be renewed. It isn't enough to simply bring up a new generation of young people in a church; there is too big of a gap in generations. New life requires new people, and connecting with them requires that we go into all the world and show them the love of Jesus.

It can be helpful to find out what unbiased impressions people in the community have of our churches. Try to learn why visitors come—and whenever possible, even be willing to ask the hard question of why visitors don't stay. These can be difficult answers to receive, but putting our heads in the sand won't help. We must ask challenging questions and be willing to accept hard answers if we want to create lasting change.

*Go* is about missions programs and overseas efforts. It's about reaching unreached people groups around the world in every way possible, from our neighbors to the farthest corners of the earth. In fact, if your church isn't giving to worldwide evangelism, I doubt that anything else I've written about will be very effective. We must help missionaries go to places where the name of Jesus isn't known, but we must also help the people in our churches to go into our backyards, our neighborhoods, and our cities. It isn't about throwing money at evangelism; it's about building relationships with people who need Jesus by bringing the presence of God everywhere we go.

## OUTWARD FOCUS

You are probably familiar with the story of the woman at the well from John 4. Jesus had a conversation with a Samaritan woman, and there are many reasons why that conversation should never have happened. He was a Jewish man; she was a Samaritan woman. He was the Son of God; she was living in sin.

But the real story may be what happened after their conversation. We read in the text that the disciples weren't present for the conversation because they were buying food in the town. When they returned from town, they saw Jesus talking to the woman but nobody asked what their conversation was about. The fact that no one even brought it up is incredible to me because it was such a striking incongruity that Jesus was talking to a Samaritan woman.

Yet nobody asked about the conversation. Why not? A very simple answer: Their minds are on something else . . . *lunch.*

They offered Jesus something to eat, but He was still focused on what had just happened. He talked to them about the harvest—it wasn't a long way off but was right in front of them.

He was saying that the kingdom of God had just walked past them on her way back into town—and they had missed it because they were focused on lunch.

We face this challenge every day. We must be careful not to have our eyes set on such a distant goal that we miss what is right in front of us. We can't be so focused on missions overseas or what we might do next year or the next that we forget the people around us who need our help today.

God wants us to engage the "women at the well" around us. This is the definition of outward focus—lifting our eyes from the distant goal in order to perceive the people already around us, near and far.

This is what *go* is all about.

# 16 WORSHIP

In Acts 2, Luke has relatively little to say about music and singing in worship, but he has a great deal to say about how the believers lived a *lifestyle* of worship. They "worshiped together at the Temple each day, met in homes for the Lord's Supper, and shared their meals with great joy and generosity—all the while praising God and enjoying the goodwill of all the people. And each day the Lord added to their fellowship those who were being saved" (Acts 2:46–47 NLT).

They worshiped together at the temple daily, and as they went about their Spirit-empowered, everyday lives they worshiped God. The results? Daily growth. God established the church as they praised Him.

When we say "worship," most pastors and many churchgoers automatically think about songs and music. While these are elements of worship, they only express one facet of a concept that is far bigger than the song service or the latest worship song topping the Christian music charts.

The word *worship* actually comes from the old English word "worthship." For us, it means living in a way that shows we value God above all else. He is worthy of our love, our loyalty, our efforts, and our courage—of everything we do each day, not just for an hour on Sunday morning.

Worship isn't an event. It's a lifestyle.

The many things we do to honor God—from singing meaningful songs, to praying, to giving, to serving—are merely expressions of worship, leaving us to ask what worship really is at its most basic. An archaic Webster's dictionary provides, perhaps, one of the best definitions I've seen by stating that worship is "to honor with extravagant love and extreme submission." Worship is less about the expressions we use and more about the heart of the one expressing them and the One to whom we give our extravagant love and extreme submission.

This isn't the book for an in-depth look at the nature of God or why He deserves our worship, but David eloquently touched on it in when he wrote, "Worship the LORD in the splendor of his holiness; tremble before him, all the earth" (Ps. 96:9 NIV). In a word, we worship God because He is *holy*. Our worship is the direct result and the only right outcome of serving a holy God, and while it may take many forms, worship is about demonstrating a sincere heart toward an unequaled God.

Quoting David again, our worship is the hunger and thirst of a soul longing for restoration to the One who created us:

O God, You are my God;
Early will I seek You;
My soul thirsts for You;
My flesh longs for You
In a dry and thirsty land
Where there is no water.
So I have looked for You in the sanctuary,
To see Your power and Your glory.
Because Your lovingkindness is better than life,
My lips shall praise You.

Thus I will bless You while I live;
I will lift up my hands in Your name.
My soul shall be satisfied as with marrow and fatness,
And my mouth shall praise You with joyful lips. (Ps. 63:1–5)

Worship is the expression of our hearts as we give glory to a holy God.

## WORSHIP IN CONTEXT

The church has gone through many phases, and in recent years, we've focused on musical worship and celebration. In some ways, this has been a good thing. In other ways, as we've focused on music, we've neglected evangelism and discipleship. Hillsong made amazing musical worship mainstream, and as it became a focus and emphasis, many churches lost the vision of the missional church and the growth of the discipling church.

With the emphasis on an emotional worship experience, we find ourselves wondering why we're producing disciples who are shallow spiritually and who live out of their emotions instead of out of the Word. When asked, average churchgoers say that the Sunday morning service is their chief source of discipleship, and in many churches, they give more time to praise and worship than to preaching or teaching of the Bible. In short, things are out of balance, and our evangelism and discipleship statistics reflect this clearly.

Worshipping God through music is a wonderful thing, but music isn't the only form of worship. The five functions God gave the first-century church were not multiple choice—we don't get to pick worship at the expense of everything else.

One of our Acts 2 team members recently visited a church in California pastored by a man whose son leads one of the most iconic Christian musical groups of the last few decades. He was surprised their musical worship lasted only ten minutes, so he asked the pastor about it afterward.

"I can't compete with my kids," he answered. "I can't buy enough lights or pump enough smoke. I can't make it enough of a concert. But church was never meant to be a concert."

He revealed that the Millennials of his church had said they were hungry for more of God's Word, and they thought the praise service was too long. "They told me they could sing anywhere, all day long," he said, "but they couldn't receive discipleship, pray with other believers, or get personalized teaching like they could in the service."

"They don't want to just get emotional about music," he went on. "They don't want to walk out not knowing anything about God's Word."

This church, which birthed an incredible musical artist, now has a short music worship time but prays together for almost fifteen minutes each service. Twenty-somethings now fill the seats and even the aisles, eagerly writing on pages of message notes or on their iPads and Smartphones, which glow in the darkened sanctuary.

In this church, the emphasis on worship through music has come full circle, swinging the emphasis around again to prayer and discipleship, which have been de-emphasized far too long.

I don't share this with you to cast a negative light on long worship services or to say that worshipping God in song isn't wonderful. However, our churches have been in the midst of a music fad for decades, and the evidence shows that we've failed to give adequate attention to making disciples who make disciples.

How can we expect to have healthy churches without a healthy perspective on worship in all its forms? That healthy perspective comes when we see worship (especially music-based worship) within a larger context of the other functions of the church. Music is just one form of worship—not the primary one.

## WORSHIP FOR THOSE WHO CAN'T SING

During our Acts 2 Journeys, we frequently bring up that the church has to be about Him and about "them"—the people outside our churches with whom we should be building relationships. The minute we get focused on us, we begin to do a lousy job of worshipping Him and an even worse job of reaching out to *them*. When we seek first the kingdom of God, He takes care of us.

As we help pastors through the Acts 2 process, we encounter many people who are looking for better answers. I mentioned earlier that the problem is that we don't need better answers; we need to ask better questions. We aren't going to get the answers we need if our questions are focused on "us."

Many churches are asking, "What kind of music will help us grow?" or "How do we keep everyone happy?" We try to shift the focus outward to ask questions like, "How can we worship God more fully?" or "How can we demonstrate God's love to people who need Him?" When we do this, the answers get much easier—and a lot more powerful for the church.

Here's a prime example of a better question: What do you do with the person in your church who doesn't sing? What does that individual do in the midst of your music?

A friend tells of an experience in his church with one such young man. He was reverent, but he didn't do what everyone else was doing during the worship time because he didn't sing. He told my friend that he didn't care about "all that other stuff" and just came to hear him preach. It really challenged my friend with the burning question of how to help this young man engage in worship.

That question created some powerful answers, one of which was that my friend started standing up at an opportune moment during the music and saying to the congregation, "Let's pause just a minute here. Finish this sentence: 'I'm so glad that God is _____.'" Then he prompted the congregation for verbal responses, and like popcorn, people began saying things out loud.

One person said they were glad that God is forgiving, another that He is merciful, and so forth. The pastor then said, "Let's take just a minute to grab on to one of these things and tell God we're glad for that. Just talk to God about it."

As they pursued answers like this to the question of what to do for people who weren't engaged in the singing, my friend watched the young man out in the congregation. He could see that in the midst of these moments, the young man was actually talking to God in a deep and meaningful way; he was worshipping God in spite of the fact that he couldn't sing. He was talking to God from his heart, and this is assuredly a deep and meaningful act of worship.

> While worship certainly includes music, it's something we can do in everyday life apart from music.

Worship is more than the ten, twenty, thirty, or however many minutes your church spends on music. While worship certainly includes music, it's something we can do in everyday life apart from music.

Worship is about how we *live*.

## REVITALIZED THROUGH PRAYER

Worship is a lifestyle, but in this age of emphasis on worship through music, many have forgotten that prayer is a powerful form of worship. One of the best ways we connect with people is speaking to them. When we speak to God, we call it "prayer"—one of the chief expressions of worship.

Worship is a tool for connecting us to God—of reaching up to our heavenly Father to ask His glory to come down. David's language of thirst and hunger that we just read from Psalms 63 is a poetic expression for the need we all have for God. That need is answered through relationship—not signs and wonders or miracles or provision, but real, organic relationship.

Worshipful prayer is nothing like the extravagant, public show the Pharisees put on to impress people. It's the urgent, honest opening of a heart to God that the tax collector showed in Jesus' parable in Luke 18. It's an expression of personal hunger. We can find amazing freedom when we worship God through prayer, hungering and thirsting for revitalization in our lives and beyond the walls of our churches.

Someone once asked British revivalist Gipsy Smith how to start a revival. He replied, "If you want to start a revival, go home and get a piece of chalk. Go into your closet and draw a circle on the floor. Kneel down in the middle of the circle and ask God to start a revival inside the chalk mark. When He has answered your prayer, the revival has begun."

Empowerment begins when you urgently seek God in worshipful prayer.

## PRAYER PREPARES YOUR HEART

You and I can't create revival, but we can pray for the power of the Spirit. We can bare our souls, simply talking with God about what concerns us, saddens us, and moves us about the condition of our nation, city, church, and ourselves.

David prayed, "Search me, O God, and know my heart; test me and know my anxious thoughts. See if there is any offensive way in me, and lead me in the way everlasting" (Ps. 139:23–24 NIV). We can prepare for a personal empowerment by asking ourselves hard questions about the condition of our hearts—and listening to the Spirit's truthful answers. Believe it or not, this type of soul-searching prayer is a form of worship.

Ask yourself where you stand with sin and repentance—are you in genuine repentance for your own sins and pursuing open accountability with trusted partners? Can you accept God's correction when you sin? Are there people who can tell you when you're wrong and you will accept what they say?

How much time do you spend in the Word? Are you feeding yourself so you'll have oil during the dry times? What about your personal devotions? Are they consistent and meaningful?

Do you harbor unforgiveness in your heart? Are you asking for forgiveness from those you have wronged? What is the condition of your heart?

What do your schedule and checkbook reveal about your priorities? Is God first? Is your relationship with your family your next priority, or have work commitments or other distractions caused you to lose your focus?

What about the fruit of the Spirit? Do you have consistent evidence that your life is producing fruit? Are you growing? Are you maturing as a disciple of Christ?

Are you as much in love with Jesus as you have ever been?

I could list another hundred questions, but the point isn't to go through a spiritual checklist in order to make yourself feel good or to reproach yourself. The point is to spur yourself on to prayer where you seek frank, honest answers from the Holy Spirit, preparing your heart for a new move of God.

Sooner or later, we all miss the boat. We slip up, fail, and falter; it's our human nature. When we do, there's only one solution: Spirit empowerment. We must repent and be restored. None of us will ever be perfect—Jesus alone pulled that off—so we don't need a system to promote perfection but one that takes us quickly to the Restorer so we can be made well in body and soul.

This is the very definition of worshipping God in prayer—and letting Him reply back to us with life-changing, Spirit-empowering words of life.

## POWERFUL PREACHING

Another element of worship is powerful preaching. Yet if we lack the power-source of the Spirit, how can we possibly deliver inspired words? Get your heart right, pray for the Spirit's empowerment, and open the doors for God to use your words as another form of worship.

Acts 2-style speaking, whether to a congregation, small group, or individuals, will create discipleship opportunities. The discipleship we demonstrate in our own lives allows us to stand before disciples who are at various points in their own faith journeys and encourage them to continue along a spiritually fruitful path. We can inspire and empower with our words, and this is surely a form of worship.

We build relationships with our words. We can connect believers to the future vision the Holy Spirit desires to speak into their lives. We can help them discover that every follower of Christ has some form of ministry calling. We can offer nuts-and-bolts discipleship through the fabric of our words, urging them to examine and fine-tune the direction of their daily lives by the power of the Spirit.

Sound like an impossible task? It is without the empowerment of the Spirit! Without Holy Spirit empowerment, we can never hope to do all of these things consistently and in a life-giving way. But when pastors, small-group leaders, and Sunday school teachers who are sensitive to the voice of the Holy Spirit worship with their words, we have a chance to bring people a message of hope. If giving words of life and hope isn't a form of honoring God through extravagant love and extreme submission, I don't know what is.

## SPIRIT-INSPIRED MUSIC

I saved music for the end of this chapter because it's the most commonly confused and clichéd understanding of worship. That isn't to diminish the importance of music—it's a vital component of preparing the congregation to receive the preaching and ministering of the Holy Spirit.

While most churches gear up for Sunday morning experiences, many have lost track of the opportunity to connect with God and with people. Our worship services can become ritualized and lose their focus on helping people to connect vertically to God while connecting horizontally with the body of believers.

Praising God through music is a timeless and peerless method for connecting at a heart level. Music elicits emotions and helps us express those emotions in our hearts. Few things can so powerfully facilitate a refreshing emotional-spiritual connection for the congregation—not to mention preparing them to receive the Word—as musical praise and worship.

I'm not going to tell you how to handle your music because every church is different. Some will spend a shorter time worshipping with music, others much longer. The point is to have a genuine expression of worship, not just a musical ritual. I've been in amazing services with only ten minutes of music and a great deal of Spirit-inspired preaching and prayer. I've also been in churches with long times of musical worship that left me hungry for God. It's all about balance. You must pray and seek the Holy Spirit's guidance to create the right balance for your congregation.

The Holy Spirit should be just as much a part of the worship service as we expect Him to be in the message. The two are interrelated and interdependent, each complementing the other. I strongly advocate leaving some flexibility in your schedule for experiencing the Holy Spirit and following His lead. Churches that are Spirit-led have an opportunity to experience God's purpose and unique direction for every moment of the worship experience.

Our worship experiences begin long before the first note is played or the first word of the message is delivered. They begin in prayer before a single person has walked through the door or the first greeter has pulled out her best smile. Similarly, they last long after the final amen; they follow people as they walk to their cars, drive away, and engage with the rest of their week.

All of these points are impossible to impact without the Holy Spirit indwelling our lives and services. We seek refreshment and connection with God and others from our worship, looking to Him to meet our hunger and provide us with hope and freedom. Yet I would argue that the primary purpose of worship is to usher in the Spirit, from empowering an individual heart to energizing an entire congregation or even a city.

We seek to give honor and glory to God through our worship as we love Him extravagantly and submit to Him completely.

That's why we raise our hands or kneel or do any of the other forms of expression that come naturally to a heart invigorated by God's Spirit—because He is our focus.

If someone in your church says he did not get anything out of the worship, it reveals an incorrect focus. It is okay to remind that person that the focus of the service is not on a personal experience but on the Holy Spirit.

Our focus is on worshipping the Lord. When we lose that focus or pick and choose which of the five functions we like best, this will impact our worship. It will also impact our ability to reach out to those beyond our churches and to maintain the outward focus that will help build the kingdom of God.

# 17 PUTTING IT ALL TOGETHER

In the course of the last five chapters, we've explored how the biblical functions from Acts 2—*connect, grow, serve, go,* and *worship*—each play a role in setting the stage for a strategic plan for your church. Each element—from the universal mission of the church to the vision God has for your church to the core values that give it a unique DNA—interacts with each of the five functions. When we explore all of these together, we can begin to form the framework of a process that is biblical, transferable, and replicable.

Whether your church is in the heart of a city, the suburbs, or in a rural area, the principles upon which Christ founded the first-century church will work, because God is the One who designed the plan. Whether your church is a small, healthy congregation or a large, struggling one, the process within Acts 2 can help your church grow in health and impact.

This is where it all comes together. You've read about the foundation upon which this is all built: every believer is a priest. You've seen that the mission Jesus gave us in the Great Commission is universal and not optional. You know that God has a plan for your church and that the Holy Spirit wants to share that vision with you. You also understand that core values represent the identity of your church and reflect how your congregation will get to that preferred future.

You build your strategic plan around the functions of the church as listed in Acts 2:42–47, which we have communicated in *connect, grow, serve, go,* and *worship.* I pray that you can use the contents of the chapter on each of these functions to begin asking the right questions for your church.

What does God say to you through each of these functions? How does your vision incorporate the mission of the church, your church's strengths, and its core values? How will you demonstrate the values (behaviors) necessary to fulfill your vision using the five functions of the first-century church? What growth steps will you take to fulfill a vision of each of the five functions over the next three to five years?

These are just a few of the primary journey points to assist your church in going to the next level. Every church will have its own unique journey to get from where you are to where you want to be, but what you have just read is the process that I lacked in my early years as a pastor.

I hope you see that the five functions I've presented are a roadmap for accomplishing our mission on earth: to make disciples, to reach the ends of the world, to develop our ministry gifts, to grow in relationships though connections, to discover how God made us, and to share our faith with others.

Remember, the five functions don't stand alone. God gave them to us to work in concert with each other at all times. They are simultaneous, not sequential. Too often, we try to separate the functions or focus on some to the exclusion of others when God intended for them to work together for our strength and harmony.

## IMPACT

The Acts 2 process is seeing results. Ninety-five percent of pastors feel better equipped to lead their congregations after going through it, and 88 percent see their teams functioning more effectively than ever before. Nearly two-thirds of declining churches who engage in an Acts 2 Journey cohort are no longer declining, and more than half are already experiencing growth.[27]

These church leaders are seeing results because they are working the process and engaging with the timeless functions upon which Jesus founded the church.

The results you experience personally hinge on your willingness to embrace change. You must decide whether or not you will accept both the Spirit's empowerment and the process God gave us in Acts 2. If you do, your church can begin to see greater impact in your community as a Spirit-empowered church with an Acts 2 vision.

## IT'S ALL ABOUT PEOPLE

Throughout the course of this book, we've been on a journey toward the next level of spiritual health. It's a process—one that continues throughout the life of a church and is renewed with new life and vision as new leaders come in and old leaders are renewed.

The journey doesn't end with this book, and it doesn't end when you craft a strategic plan for your church that uses the five functions as a template. As you grow and the church grows, as leaders come and go, and as society changes, the need for reviewing this process will come again and again.

One thing will never change: This is all about *people*.

The church isn't a building. *You and your people are the church.* But you are more than the church and the hope of the world . . . you are the *Spirit-empowered church*, and you have exactly what a lost and hurting world needs most. Now, it's time for you to put all of this together and use it for your church. It's time to train the next generation of disciples and equip the saints for the work of the ministry, for we are all truly part of a royal priesthood of believers!

# EPILOGUE
## HOPE FOUND

--------------------------------------------------------------

Across America and the world, churches and church leaders are looking for hope. We want to be relevant and effective, and we want to leave a powerful legacy of hope for future generations. The choices we make today will shape the church of tomorrow.

Will it be strong, or will it be crumbling?

We haven't lost our faith—we still believe in the truth of God's Word, the Great Commission, and the Great Commandment. We still believe in the power of the Holy Spirit, and our hearts still yearn to see God's kingdom advance on the earth.

But all too often what we have lost is our *hope.*

In my own life, I stared this in the face as my mom, such a longstanding anchor of faith and hope for our family, pointed her finger in my face and told me never to pray in her presence again. It reduced me to tears as I drove home and later as I prayed that night.

My dad lay near death, had not spoken a word in months, and had not been coherent in years. Though he and my mom had ministered to many people and had seen many great moves of God, all of our prayers for Dad seemed to have gone unanswered.

It had taken a great toll on my mom.

I was afraid she had lost her faith, but in my tearful prayers that night, the Holy Spirit showed me the truth: She hadn't lost her faith at all. Her decades of service to Christ had forged in her a faith that would never be lost. She knew in her mind that God's promises are true . . . but in her despair, she had lost hope.

## FINAL WORD

Four days after my mother's angry, bitter, and hopeless outburst, she went back to the hospital to visit Dad. There, to her astonishment, she felt the presence of God.

"I didn't want to feel it," she told me later, "but it was like an anointing cloud."

In the Old Testament, they called it the Shekinah glory. God is so powerfully real that He has an essence about Him we can sometimes sense. It was this essence of God's Spirit that came over my mother when she walked into Dad's room—and accompanying that essence, she heard a voice speak to her heart.

Four days earlier, I had heard the voice of the Enemy trying to destroy my hope, but this day, the voice of the Holy Spirit whispered to my mother.

He said, *"Get ready; he's going to talk to you today."*

That was crazy! The doctors had already told us Dad was gone. Even if he came out of the coma, it had been months since he had spoken. His speech leading up to this crisis had been unintelligible for months.

My mother had lost all hope, but the voice of the Spirit was nudging her hope gauge just a little bit and it began to swell from empty to full. She sat down by Dad's bed and waited with anticipation for what he would say.

"I don't know if I waited three minutes or three hours," she told me later, "but I was looking into his eyes when they cleared up, and he looked right at me." Her own eyes glowed as she told me, "His mouth began to move, and with a strong voice he said, 'You know what, honey? God still answers prayer.'"

For the next ten minutes, my dad lay there, praying in an unknown tongue under the power of the Holy Spirit. Finally, he slid back into the coma.

Soon afterward, he died.

"Son, nobody else could have spoken that phrase to me," my mother declared afterward. "Not you, not any preacher, not any prophet—nobody could have spoken that phrase and had it mean anything to me. The only man who could say that and have it mean anything to me was your daddy, and he was brain-dead— but God let him preach one more message! And it restored my hope!"

## THE HOPE OF THE WORLD

Today, we stand at a crossroads in our culture and in our churches. The Devil wants to stop the church, and to do that, he tries to take us out individually. He knows it's easier to prey on our emotions than it is to defeat us scripturally, so he manipulates the way we think about our circumstances to make it appear that hope is lost.

However, he can't alter the Word of God, and he can't resist the power of the Holy Spirit.

God shares a process in Acts 2 that offers any church hope, because it's His original blueprint. In our shifting, changing world, God's Word remains, and His plan for the original church hasn't changed to fit the times. It's as timeless as our mission.

God has given us His Word so we might stand firm and have hope. Paul tells us, "For whatever was written in earlier times was written for our instruction, so that through perseverance and the encouragement of the Scriptures we might have hope" (Rom. 15:4 NASB). And in another place, he writes, "Three things will last forever—faith, hope, and love" (1 Cor. 13:13 NLT).

The Devil can try. He can lie, he can cheat, he can steal—but in the end, he doesn't have the authority to take our hope.

So we must not give it to him.

My father's miraculous final words restored my mother's hope. As you face the challenges of leading a church, what will restore your hope, friend?

Trying times have come before, and the Lord has graciously breathed life over the coals, bringing revitalization just when it seemed all was lost. Just as He breathed life into humankind and upon those gathered in the Upper Room, His breath of life is all that is necessary for us to spring up into flame again! He yearns to empower His church and see us make a great impact on our world!

It has happened before, and great moves of God have swept across the face of the world to push back tides of darkness. If it has happened before, it can happen again. But we must pray for it and seek His empowerment.

The gates of hell will not prevail against the Spirit-empowered church God placed on this earth to win the lost. May we be found doing this mission faithfully and be told, "Well done, good and faithful servants."

So where do we look to restore our hope? New ministry strategies? Old traditions recovered?

No. We can't look to our own ingenuity, intellect, and human effort. Our hope isn't in a program or even a process—it's in a Person.

Hundreds of years before Christ, Isaiah prophesied a word that Jesus fulfilled. Matthew records the fulfillment of the prophetic word:

He will not crush the weakest reed
or put out a flickering candle.
Finally he will cause justice to be victorious.
And his name will be the hope
of all the world. (Matt. 12:20–21 NLT)

We have hope because we have Jesus. Now, let us give that hope away to the lost people of this world as a church empowered by the very Spirit that raised Christ from the dead.

# ENDNOTES

1   This figure comes from our denomination's statistician and is derived from reports submitted by our churches. We calculate a church is declining if it has decreased by more than 10 percent in a five-year period. Similarly, a church with less than a 10 percent growth over five years is classified as plateaued.

2   Dave Kinnaman, *unChristian* (Grand Rapids: Baker Book House, 2007), 79.

3   www.albertmohler.com/category/blog/

4   George Bullard Jr., *Seven Enduring Principles for Transforming Your Congregation*, The Columbia Partnership, 2009 accessed August 1, 2016, http://columbiapartnership.typepad.com/files/seven -enduring-principles-for-transforming-your-congregation.doc

5   Denzil Miller, *The Spirit of God in Missions* (Springfield, MO: PneumaLife Publications, 2012), 233.

6   Stephen R Covey, A. Roger Merrill, and Rebecca R. Merrill, *First Things First Every Day* (Wichita, KS: Fireside Publishing, 1997), 103.

7   Cited by Gerardo Marti, *A Mosaic of Believers* (Bloomington, IN: Indiana University Press, 2009), 78.

8   Aubrey Malphurs, *Ministry Nuts and Bolts* (Grand Rapids, MI: Kregel, 2009), 17.

9   Christian A. Schwarz, *Natural Church Development* (Carol Stream, IL: ChurchSmart Resources, 1996). Cited in *Cell Church Magazine*, Fall 1997.

10 Cited by Kelly Shattuck in "7 Startling Facts: An Up Close Look at Church Attendance in America," *ChurchLeaders*, www.churchleaders.com/pastors/pastor-articles/139575-7-startling-facts-an-up-close-look-at-church-attendance-in-america.html.

11 Larry Crabb, *Connecting* (Nashville: Thomas Nelson, 1997), Epub Kindle Loc. 128.

12 Crabb, *Connecting*, Epub Kindle Loc. 3792.

13 Crabb, *Connecting*, Epub Kindle Loc. 93.

14 David Olson, *The American Church in Crisis* (Grand Rapids, MI: Zondervan, 2008), 137.

15 Dr. David Ferguson, *Relational Foundations* (Austin, TX: Relationship Press, 2004) 72–74.

16 Dr. David Ferguson, *Relational Discipleship*, (Austin, TX: Relationship Press, 2005), 96.

17 Leonard Sweet, *Giving Blood* (Grand Rapids, MI: Zondervan, 2014), 46.

18 Ibid., 47.

19 Ibid., 300.

20 Ibid., 251.

21 Ibid., 54.

22 Cited by Robert E. Webber, *Journey to Jesus* (Nashville: Abington Press, 2001), 11–15.

23 Ferguson, *Relational Foundations*, 153.

24 Ron Bennett, *Intentional Disciplemaking* (Colorado Springs, CO: NavPress, 2001), 12–13.

25 Thom Ranier, *The Unchurched Next Door* (Grand Rapids: Zondervan, 2003), cited by backtochurch.com/participate/resources/statistics.

26 Ibid.

27 These statistics are based on outcome studies from our Acts 2 Journey churches.

# APPENDIX

## FORTY INDICATORS OF A SPIRIT-EMPOWERED DISCIPLE

Many leaders in our Acts 2 Journeys have asked for a comprehensive list of the characteristics of a Spirit-empowered disciple. There has only been one person who loved God with all His heart, soul, and mind and loved His neighbor as Himself, but God wants all of us to keep growing in faith, love, hope, and character. You can use this list of forty indicators as an assessment of strengths and areas that need attention, but always encourage people to see themselves in the process of growth. We will only "arrive" in the new heaven and new earth! (All Scriptures below are taken from the New American Standard version of the Bible.)

### A Spirit-empowered disciple loves the Lord through . . .

### 1. Practicing thanksgiving in all things

*"Enter His gates with thanksgiving" (Ps. 100:4). "In everything give thanks" (1 Thess. 5:18). "As sorrowful yet always rejoicing" (2 Cor. 6:10).*

### 2. Listening to God for direction and discernment

*"Speak* LORD, *Your servant is listening" (1 Sam. 3:9). "She had a sister called Mary, who was seated at the Lord's feet, listening to His word" (Luke 10:39). "Shall I hide from Abraham what I am about to do" (Gen. 18:17)? "His anointing teaches you about all things" (1 John 2:27).*

### 3. Experiencing God as He really is through deepened intimacy with Him

*"Hear, O Israel! The* LORD *is our God, the* LORD *is one. You shall love the* LORD *your God with all your heart and with all your soul and with all your might" (Deut. 6:4). "The* LORD *longs to be gracious to you, and therefore He waits on high to have compassion on you. For the* LORD *is a God of justice" (Isa. 30:18). See also John 14:9.*

### 4. Rejoicing regularly in His identity as "His Beloved"

*"His banner over me is love" (Song. 2:4). "To the praise of the glory of His grace, which He freely bestowed on us in the Beloved" (Eph. 1:6). "He gives to His beloved even in his sleep" (Ps. 127:2).*

### 5. Living with a passionate longing for purity and to please God in all things

*"Who may ascend the hill of the* LORD? . . . *He who has clean hands and a pure heart" (Ps. 24:3–4). "Let us cleanse ourselves from all defilement of flesh and spirit, perfecting holiness in the fear of God" (2 Cor. 7:1). "I always do the things that are pleasing to Him" (John 8:29). "Though He slay me, I will hope in Him" (Job 13:15).*

### 6. Consistent practice of self-denial, fasting, and solitude rest

*"He turned and said to Peter, 'Get behind me, Satan! You are a stumbling block to Me; for you are not setting your mind on God's interests, but man's'" (Matt. 16:23). "But you, when you fast, anoint your head and wash your face." (Matt. 6:17). "Cease striving and know that I am God" (Ps. 46:10).*

### 7. Entering often into Spirit-led praise and worship

*"Bless the LORD O my soul, and all that is within me, bless His holy name." (Ps. 103:1). "Worship the LORD with reverence and rejoice with trembling" (Ps. 2:11). "I praise You, Father, Lord of heaven and earth . . ." (Matt. 11:25).*

### 8. Disciplined, bold, and believing prayer

*"Pray at all times in the Spirit" (Eph. 6:18). "Call to Me and I will answer you . . ." (Jer. 33:3)). "If we ask anything according to His will, He hears us. . . . We know that we have the requests which we have asked from Him" (1 John 5:14–15).*

### 9. Yielding to the Spirit's fullness as life in the Spirit brings supernatural intimacy with the Lord, manifestation of divine gifts, and witness of the fruit of the Spirit

*"For by one Spirit we were all baptized into one body, whether Jews or Greeks, whether slaves or free, and we were all made to drink of one Spirit" (1 Cor. 12:13). "You will receive power when the Holy Spirit has come upon you" (Acts 1:8). "But to each one is given the manifestation of the Spirit for the common good" (1 Cor. 12:7). See also 1 Peter 4:10 and Romans 12:6.*

10. Practicing the presence of the Lord; yielding to the Spirit's work of Christ-likeness

*"But we all, with unveiled face, beholding as in a mirror the glory of the Lord, are being transformed into the same image from glory to glory, just as from the Lord, the Spirit"* (2 Cor. 3:18). *"As the deer pants for the water brooks, so my soul pants after You, O God"* (Ps. 42:1).

## A Spirit-empowered disciple loves the Word through . . .

### 1. Frequently being led by the Spirit into deeper love for the One who wrote the Word

*"You shall love the Lord your God with all your heart, and with all your soul, and with all your mind. . . . You shall love your neighbor as yourself. On these two commandments depend the whole Law and the Prophets"* (Matt. 22:37–39). *"I shall delight in Your commands, which I love."* (Ps. 119:47). *"The judgments of the* Lord *are true; they are righteous altogether. They are more desirable than gold . . . sweeter also than honey"* (Ps. 19:9–10).

### 2. Being a "living epistle" in reverence and awe as His Word becomes real in my life, vocation, and calling

*"You are our letter, written in our hearts, known and read by all men"* (2 Cor. 3:2). *"And the Word became flesh and dwelt among us"* (John 1:14). *"Husbands, love your wives . . . having cleansed her by the washing of water with the Word"* (Eph. 5:26). *"Whatever you do, do your work heartily, as for the Lord"* (Col. 3:23). See also Titus 2:5.

### 3. Yielding to the Scripture's protective cautions and transforming power to bring life change in myself

*"From Your precepts I get understanding; therefore I hate every false way" (Ps. 119:104). "May it be done to me according to your word" (Luke 1:38). "How can a young man keep his way pure? By keeping it according to Your word" (Ps. 119:9). See also Colossians 3:16–17.*

### 4. Humbly and vulnerably sharing of the Spirit's transforming work through the Word

*"I will speak of your testimonies before kings and shall not be ashamed" (Ps. 119:46). "Preach the word; be ready in season and out of season" (2 Tim. 4:2).*

### 5. Meditating consistently on more and more of the Word hidden in the heart

*"Your Word I have treasured in my heart, that I may not sin against You" (Ps. 119:11). "Let the words of my mouth and the meditation of my heart be acceptable in Your sight, O LORD, my rock and my Redeemer" (Ps. 19:14).*

### 6. Encountering Jesus in the Word for deepened transformation in Christ-likeness

*"But we all, with unveiled face, beholding as in a mirror the glory of the Lord, are being transformed into the same image from glory to glory, just as from the Lord, the Spirit" (2 Cor. 3:18). "If you abide in Me, and My words abide in you, ask whatever you wish, and it will be done for you" (John 15:7). See also Luke 24:32; Psalm 119:136; and 2 Corinthians 1:20.*

### 7. A life explained as one of "experiencing Scripture"

*"This is what was spoken of by the prophet Joel" (Acts 2:16). "This is my comfort in my affliction, that Your word has revived me" (Ps. 119:50). "My soul is crushed with longing after Your ordinances at all times" (Ps. 119:20).*

### 8. Living "naturally supernatural" in all of life as His Spirit makes the written Word (*logos*) the living Word (*Rhema*)

*"Faith comes from hearing, and hearing by the word [Rhema] of Christ" (Rom. 10:17). "Your word is a lamp to my feet and a light to my path" (Ps. 119:105).*

### 9. Living abundantly "in the present" as His Word brings healing to hurt, anger, guilt, fear, and condemnation—which are heart hindrances to life abundant

*"The thief comes only to steal and kill and destroy" (John 10:10). "I shall run the way of Your commandments, for You will enlarge my heart" (Ps. 119:32). "You will know the truth, and the truth will make you free" (John. 8:32). "It was for freedom that Christ set us free; therefore keep standing firm and do not be subject again to a yoke of slavery" (Gal. 5:1).*

### 10. Implicit, unwavering trust that His Word will never fail

*"The grass withers, the flower fades, but the word of our God stands forever" (Isa. 40:8). "So will My word be which goes forth from My mouth, it will not return to Me empty" (Isa. 55:11).*

A Spirit-empowered disciple loves people through . . .

**1. Living a Spirit-led life of doing good in all of life: relationships and vocation, community and calling**

*"He went about doing good" (Acts 10:38). "Let your light shine before men in such a way that they may see your good works, and glorify your Father who is in heaven" (Matt. 5:16). "But love your enemies, and do good, and lend, expecting nothing in return; and your reward will be great, and you will be sons of the Most High; for He Himself is kind to ungrateful and evil men" (Luke 6:35). See also Romans 15:2.*

**2. "Startling people" with loving initiatives to "give first"**

*"Give, and it will be given to you. They will pour into your lap a good measure—pressed down, shaken together, and running over. For by your standard of measure it will be measured to you in return" (Luke 6:38). "But Jesus was saying, 'Father, forgive them; for they do not know what they are doing'" (Luke 23:34). See also Luke 23:43 and John 19:27.*

**3. Discerning the relational needs of others with a heart to give of His love**

*"Let no unwholesome word proceed from your mouth, but only such a word as is good for edification according to the need of the moment, so that it will give grace to those who hear" (Eph. 4:29). "And my God will supply all your needs according to His riches in glory in Christ Jesus" (Phil. 4:19). See also Luke 6:30.*

**4. Seeing people as needing both redemption from sin and intimacy in relationships, addressing both human fallenness and aloneness**

*"But God demonstrates His own love toward us, in that while we were yet sinners, Christ died for us" (Rom. 5:8). "When Jesus came to the place, He looked up and said to him, 'Zacchaeus, hurry and come down, for today I must stay at your house'" (Luke 19:5). See also Mark 8:24 and Genesis 2:18.*

**5. Ministering His life and love to our nearest ones at home and with family as well as faithful engagement in His body, the church**

*"You husbands in the same way, live with your wives in an understanding way, as with someone weaker, since she is a woman; and show her honor as a fellow heir of the grace of life, so that your prayers will not be hindered" (1 Peter 3:7). See also 1 Peter 3:1 and Psalm 127:3.*

**6. Expressing the fruit of the Spirit as a lifestyle and identity**

*"But the fruit of the Spirit is love, joy, peace, patience, kindness, goodness, faithfulness, gentleness, self-control" (Gal. 5:22–23). "With the fruit of a man's mouth his stomach will be satisfied; he will be satisfied with the product of his lips" (Prov. 18:20).*

**7. Expecting and demonstrating the supernatural as His spiritual gifts are made manifest and His grace is at work by His Spirit**

*"In the power of signs and wonders, in the power of the Spirit; so that from Jerusalem and round about as far as Illyricum I have fully preached the gospel of Christ" (Rom. 15:19). "Truly, truly, I say*

to you, he who believes in Me, the works that I do, he will do also" *(John 14:12). See also 1 Corinthians 14:1.*

## 8. Taking courageous initiative as a peacemaker, reconciling relationships along life's journey

*"Live in peace with one another" (1 Thess. 5:13). "For He Himself is our peace, who made both groups into one and broke down the barrier of the dividing wall" (Eph. 2:14). "Therefore, confess your sins to one another, and pray for one another so that you may be healed" (James 5:16). See also Ephesians 4:31–32.*

## 9. Demonstrating His love to an ever growing network of "others" as He continues to challenge us to love "beyond our comfort zone"

*"The one who says, 'I have come to know Him,' and does not keep His commandments, is a liar, and the truth is not in him" (1 John 2:4). "If someone says, 'I love God,' and hates his brother, he is a liar; for the one who does not love his brother whom he has seen, cannot love God whom he has not seen" (1 John 4:20).*

## 10. Humbly acknowledging to the Lord, ourselves, and others that it is Jesus in and through us who is loving others at their point of need

*"Take My yoke upon you and learn from Me, for I am gentle and humble in heart, and you will find rest for your souls" (Matt. 11:29). "If I then, the Lord and the Teacher, washed your feet, you also ought to wash one another's feet" (John 13:14).*

A Spirit-empowered disciple loves His mission through . . .

### 1. Imparting the gospel and one's very life in daily activities and relationships, vocation, and community

*"Having so fond an affection for you, we were well-pleased to impart to you not only the gospel of God but also our own lives, because you had become very dear to us" (1 Thess. 2:8–9). See also Ephesians 6:19.*

### 2. Expressing and extending the kingdom of God as compassion, justice, love, and forgiveness are shared

*"I must preach the kingdom of God to the other cities also, for I was sent for this purpose" (Luke 4:43). "As You sent Me into the world, I also have sent them into the world" (John 17:18). "Restore to me the joy of Your salvation and sustain me with a willing spirit. Then I will teach transgressors Your ways, and sinners will be converted to you" (Ps. 51:12–13). See also Micah 6:8.*

### 3. Championing Jesus as the only hope of eternal life and abundant living

*"There is salvation in no one else; for there is no other name under heaven that has been given among men by which we must be saved" (Acts 4:12). "The thief comes only to steal and kill and destroy; I came that they may have life, and have it abundantly" (John 10:10). See also Acts 4:12; John 10:10 and 14:6.*

### 4. Yielding to the Spirit's role to convict others as He chooses; resisting expressions of condemnation

*"And He, when He comes, will convict the world concerning sin and righteousness and judgment" (John 16:8). "Who is the one who*

condemns? Christ Jesus is He who died, yes, rather who was raised, who is at the right hand of God, who also intercedes for us" (Rom. 8:34). See also Romans 8:1.

## 5. Ministering His life and love to the "least of these"

"Then He will answer them, 'Truly I say to you, to the extent that you did not do it to one of the least of these, you did not do it to Me'" (Matt. 25:45). "Pure and undefiled religion in the sight of our God and Father is this: to visit orphans and widows in their distress, and to keep oneself unstained by the world" (James 1:27).

## 6. Bearing witness of a confident peace and expectant hope in God's lordship in all things

"Now may the Lord of peace Himself continually grant you peace in every circumstance. The Lord be with you all" (2 Thess. 3:16)! "Let the peace of Christ rule in your hearts, to which indeed you were called in one body; and be thankful" (Col. 3:15). See also Romans 8:28 and Psalm 146:5.

## 7. Faithfully sharing of time, talents, gifts, and resources in furthering His mission

"Of this church I was made a minister according to the stewardship from God bestowed on me for your benefit, so that I might fully carry out the preaching of the word of God" (Col. 1:25). "From everyone who has been given much, much will be required; and to whom they entrusted much, of him they will ask all the more" (Luke 12:48). See also 1 Corinthians 4:1–2.

## 8. Attentive listening to others' stories, vulnerably sharing of our story, and a sensitive witness of Jesus' story as life's ultimate hope

*"But sanctify Christ as Lord in your hearts, always being ready to make a defense to everyone who asks you to give an account for the hope that is in you, yet with gentleness and reverence"* (1 Peter 3:15). *"This son of mine was dead and has come to life again"* (Luke 15:24). See also Mark 5:21–42 and John 9:1–35.

## 9. Pouring our life into others and making disciples who in turn make disciples of others

*"Go therefore and make disciples of all nations, baptizing them in the name of the Father and the Son and the Holy Spirit, teaching them to observe all that I commanded you; and lo, I am with you always, even to the end of the age"* (Matt. 28:19–20). See also 2 Timothy 2:2.

## 10. Living submissively within His body the church as instruction, encouragement, reproof, and correction are graciously received from faithful disciples

*"Be subject to one another in the fear of Christ"* (Eph. 5:21). *"Brethren, even if anyone is caught in any trespass, you who are spiritual, restore such a one in a spirit of gentleness; each one looking to yourself, so that you too will not be tempted"* (Gal. 6:1). See also Galatians 6:2.

# ACKNOWLEDGEMENTS

I'm extremely grateful to everyone who has made a contribution to this book.

To Johanna—your wise counsel and constant support helped shape our ministerial journey that formed many of the principles found here.

To the Acts 2 Journey team—Mike Clarensau, Ron McManus, and Rick Allen—collectively and individually, you have helped provide the outline, process, and testimonials. Your experiences as facilitators of the Acts 2 Journey with scores of churches have turned theory into verifiable outcomes.

To First Assembly of God, North Little Rock, Arkansas—thanks for your patience and support. You were the laboratory for the principles in this book and a testimony that the biblical model from Acts 2:42–47 can develop a healthy, vibrant, growing, missional church.

To Pastor Rod Loy—thanks for helping develop, discover, and discern many of these principles as we partnered together as team members at First Assembly of God, North Little Rock. Your keen insights and input helped bring *connect, grow, serve, go,* and *worship* into a workable model. As the successor to my leadership at First NLR, you have demonstrated that the foundation you helped develop was strong enough to support higher peaks than either of us could have imagined.

To Jackie Chrisner and Kristen Speer—thanks for helping me stay on track and tie up all the loose ends. There are so many details surrounding this project, and I could never have gotten everything done without your help.

To the publishing team—thanks for believing that this book can help other leaders to develop and lead Spirit-empowered churches.

# ABOUT THE AUTHOR

-------------------------------------------------------------------

Alton Garrison serves as the director of the Acts 2 Journey Initiative which helps churches renew their spiritual vitality and reach their full kingdom potential.

Garrison served as assistant general superintendent of the Assemblies of God from 2007–19, as executive director of U.S. Missions from 2005–07, as superintendent of the Arkansas district from 2001–05, as pastor of First Assembly of God, North Little Rock, Arkansas, from 1986–2001, and as an evangelist from 1968–1985.

In addition, he is the chair of PCCNA (Pentecostal Charismatic Churches of North America) as well as the chair of the WAGF (World Assemblies of God Fellowship) Revitalization Commission.

Garrison and his wife, Johanna, have one daughter, Lizette, one grandson, and one granddaughter. He has authored the books: *Hope in America's Crisis, Building a Winning Team, Acts 2 Church*, and *The 360° Disciple*. Johanna authored the book, *Tangled Destinies*, an account of her family's hardships through the Holocaust carried out by the Nazis in World War II and an Indonesian revolution, and their subsequent immigration to the United States.

Alton and Johanna currently reside in Springfield, Missouri.